I0824394

the little book of crystals

the little book of crystals

EASY WAYS TO TRANSFORM YOUR LIFE

golnaz alibagi

CICO BOOKS

To my three favorite people in the world: my mum, dad, and sister who I love with all my heart.

Published in 2026 by CICO Books
an imprint of Ryland Peters & Small Ltd
20–21 Jockey's Fields 1452 Davis Bugg Road
London WC1R 4BW Warrenton, NC 27589
www.rylandpeters.com
Email: euregulations@rylandpeters.com

Adapted from *The Essential Guide to Crystals*, first published in 2014

10 9 8 7 6 5 4 3 2 1

A CIP record for this book is available from the British Library.
US Library of Congress CIP data has been applied for.

ISBN: 978-1-80065-646-8

Printed in China

Photographers: Geoff Dann and Roy Palmer
Editors: Marion Paull and Imogen Valler-Miles
Senior designer: Emily Breen
Art director: Sally Powell
Creative director: Leslie Harrington
Production manager: Gordana Simakovic
Publishing manager: Carmel Edmonds

The authorised representative in the EEA is
Authorised Rep Compliance Ltd.,
Ground Floor. 71 Lower Baggot Street,
Dublin, D01 P593, Ireland
www.arccompliance.com

SAFETY NOTE

Please note that while the descriptions of the properties of crystals refer to healing benefits, they are not intended to replace diagnosis of illness or ailments, or healing or medicine. Always consult your doctor or other health professional in the case of illness.

contents

introduction

Welcome to your essential, no-fuss guide to attracting everything you've ever wanted using crystals. Whether you're hoping to attract your dream partner, job, or home, wish to maximize your bank balance, career success, or natural beauty (yes, really!), or simply want to fall in love with yourself and life again there's a gem for you.

The tips are categorized by area of life. Most pages provide simple, single-crystal tips while other pages provide an in-depth look at a particular issue or scenario and discuss numerous crystals that will help. "Power crystal" pages shine a spotlight on some key gems in the crystal world, sharing a little bit of lore: their corresponding star signs, planets, elements,

and chakras (see page 132), as well as "gem-scriptions" and "crystal cocktail" ideas for combining crystals to maximize their healing power.

Of course, in today's busy world, with children, jobs, and social engagements to keep up with, it can be hard to find the time, money, or energy for long-winded rituals. I've found the quickest and easiest rituals for you to try. Nothing in this book will take you longer than 15 minutes and, better still, most of the tips involve nothing more than wearing one of the gems around your neck.

Prepare for the start of a truly breathtaking adventure that will lead you straight to your happily ever after.

getting started

Before we start our journey together, it's important to know how to choose the right crystals. See opposite for a quick guide. As your crystal collection grows, you may find that you go through phases when some gems don't feel like a good match for you any longer. This is perfectly natural. Some gems are destined to be our lifelong companions, while others will only be with us for a short time. There may even be some crystals that we form on-off relationships with!

It's easy to look after your gems and, with just a little bit of time and attention, your crystals will work with you for many years, growing in power over time. To prepare your crystals, you will need to cleanse them to keep them supercharged with healing energy—see pages 10–11.

choosing the right crystals

This is very much like packing for a holiday; certain outfits (aka gems) will suit particular occasions, and what might work for someone else may not be right for you. Here are a few tips to help you find the right crystal.

1

Look up your dilemma, and see which of the suggested gems you're instantly drawn to.

2

Hold this book in your hands, focus on your dilemma, and ask the gems for guidance. Open it randomly, and the first crystal you notice will lead you to the answer.

3

Spread a few gems on a table (or go to a crystal shop) and hover your hands over the gemstones. Ask them for help, and you'll soon notice your hands naturally gravitate toward one (or feel a warm sensation over it). You can also do this by opening this book on a specific chapter and holding your hands over the page.

cleansing a crystal

Once you've found the right gem, you should cleanse it regularly (as you would an outfit) to clear any nasty stains (aka negative energy) from the past. Generally speaking, you should have a "laundry day" once a month, or after any ritual you've completed. Make it fun by dedicating a whole day or afternoon to it, and use the power of the elements to help you. You can either pick the element you're most drawn to, go for the element associated with your star sign, or rotate them depending on the season (i.e. water for winter, fire for summer).

water

Hold your crystal under running water for a few minutes, and leave it to dry naturally. (Note: some gems are water-soluble so avoid this method if yours isn't water-friendly. If your gem is porous or has a high metal content, don't cleanse it using water, use one of the other methods described.)

earth

Bury your crystal in some soil (either in your garden, or a plant pot) and leave it there for 24 hours. You can also do this on a full moon, and leave it there until a new one.

fire

Light some incense, and waft its smoke over your gemstone for five minutes. Scents that work particularly well are sage, frankincense, sandalwood, juniper, pine, and rose. Make sure that your crystal does not get too hot or it will crack.

air

Leave your crystal under the light of a full or new moon overnight, or under sunlight for a few hours. (Note: some crystals fade or catch fire in the sun, so try a different method unless you're absolutely certain. Crystals that shouldn't be cleansed using this method include Amethyst, Smoky Quartz, and Chrysocolla, among others.)

CHAPTER ONE

love and romance

Find your soulmate, transform your relationship, and learn to love yourself

finding love

PEARL

Accepting love Prepare yourself to be romance-ready by holding a Pearl by your heart. The gem will clear away any negative beliefs that are preventing you from accepting love, such as unworthiness, doubt, or fear, and prepare you to catch Cupid's arrow.

Alternative gemstones
Rhodochrosite, Honey Opal, Celestite.

RHODOCHROSITE

Attracting a new partner Boost your sex appeal by placing a piece of Rhodochrosite in your bra or pocket (or simply holding one close to your heart) to maximize your attractiveness to those around you, and help you mesmerize everyone you meet.

Alternative gemstones
Amber, Imperial Topaz, Sunstone.

PINK TOURMALINE

Empowerment Learn how to fall in love without being subsumed by holding a Pink Tourmaline by your heart to help you feel happy, contented, and whole—with or without someone at home.

Alternative gemstones
Pink Halite, Rhodonite, Uvarovite Garnet.

Anxiety about love Open your heart to love as though it's never been broken by holding a Watermelon Tourmaline. The gem will prevent your previous heartaches from tainting your faith in fairy-tale romances, and ensure you never lose hope in your happy ending.

WATERMELON TOURMALINE

Alternative gemstones

Celestite, Sunstone, Dioptase.

Chasing away singleton blues Chasing love is a bit like trying to catch a butterfly—the more you grasp at it, the farther away it flies. Wear an Abalone Shell to help you feel less lonely without a partner, and inspire you to stop chasing butterflies and wait for the one who gives them to you.

ABALONE SHELL

Alternative gemstones

Mangano Calcite, Watermelon Tourmaline, Rose Quartz.

First-date confidence Ease into your first date by keeping a Zircon in your pocket to enhance your personal magnetism, and ensure the only thing running away from you is the time!

ZIRCON

Alternative gemstones

Hematite, Imperial Topaz, Boulder Opal.

ROSE QUARTZ

Being spontaneous In a world where mere chance can lead to wedding bells, you never know what's going to happen. You could walk out of your house, trip, fall, and land yourself a spouse! Hold a Rose Quartz to attract love into your life.

Alternative gemstones
Rutilated Topaz, Rhodochrosite, Pink Tourmaline.

EUDIALYTE

Opening your heart to love When we have been burned by the fire of love, many of us allow our hearts to become cold. We refuse to believe that we can love again after a failed romance. Freeze a few rose petals, hold a Eudialyte, and watch the petals melt to prevent your heart from staying frozen.

Alternative gemstones
Yellow Crackle Quartz, Roselite, Pink Tourmaline.

MERLINITE

Don't be a cynic It's never too late to meet your perfect mate. Affirm this to yourself by hanging a heart pendant on a chain with a Merlinite any time you start feeling skeptical. This will remind you that it's very often when we're at our most cynical that love turns around and hands us a miracle.

Alternative gemstones
Marble, Chrysoberyl, Iceland Spar.

Finding love in your later years "Nothing in nature is hurried, yet everything is accomplished." Lao Tzu's maxim also applies to true love. You can't judge a seed before it's been sown, or hurry a flower to bloom. Hold a Green Aventurine to help you patiently await love's arrival.

GREEN AVENTURINE

Alternative gemstones
Morganite, Pink Tourmaline, Rose Quartz.

Find a last-minute date Looking for a date as your plus-one for a special event? Simply wear a Morganite around your neck for a few days before the big event, and you can be sure you won't be turning up alone!

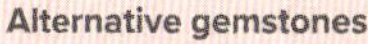

Alternative gemstones
Rose Quartz, Ruby, Blue Aragonite.

MORGANITE

Know that you are already whole Relationships aren't about finding someone to complete you; if you've got a mind, body, and soul, you're already whole. Wear a Lepidolite to help you overcome your timidity on dates, and realize that a soulmate's a mate for the soul, not someone to make it whole.

Alternative gemstones
Rhodonite, Iolite, Vera Cruz Amethyst.

LEPIDOLITE

looking for love

First you have to learn to love yourself. Otherwise, looking for love is like going shopping without a purse—pointless, painful, and guaranteed to end in tears. When you feel ready for a new relationship, give your heart an emotional detox by holding a piece of **Chrysocolla** to help you draw a line under previous disappointments. Wearing a **Pink Danburite** will help ensure your most valuable accessory—self-love—is in abundant supply.

Then create a vision board and fill it with images of your ideal mate. Be specific and include all the lovely things you would like to do together. Look at it each night with a **Pink Tourmaline** by your heart. You could also give Cupid a nudge by writing a list of all the things you're looking for in a partner, and reading it each night with a **Blue Aragonite** by your heart to help you visualize someone sweeping you off your feet.

A quieter way to discover your romantic fate is to spend five minutes holding a **Rose Quartz** just before you go to bed, and asking it to show you, while you sleep, who you're destined to meet. Then, your ritual of choice performed, snuggle down, knowing that sweet dreams of your future lover await you.

PINK DANBURITE

PINK TOURMALINE

CHRYSOCOLLA

alternative gemstones

Chrysocolla Agate, Rhodonite, Larimar.

Pink Danburite Shift Quartz, Tugtupite, Pink Crackle Quartz.

Pink Tourmaline Roselite, Rose Quartz, Morganite.

Blue Aragonite Rose Quartz, Morganite, Imperial Topaz.

Rose Quartz Bowenite, Blue Howlite, Molybdenite.

BLUE ARAGONITE

ROSE QUARTZ

coupled up

GREEN TOURMALINE

Communication in relationships Breathe new life into your relationship by placing a Green Tourmaline crystal in a potted plant, and leaving it beside a photo of you and your partner. The gem is said to encourage growth in everything—from romance and finances to shrubbery!—and will help your love blossom.

Alternative gemstones
Kyanite, Aquamarine, Larimar.

BLUE CHALCEDONY

Express your emotions Hold a Blue Chalcedony by your throat to help you speak from your heart, and give you the courage to reveal your deepest thoughts and emotions, rather than keeping them hidden.

Alternative gemstones
Blue Quartz, Cobaltoan Calcite, Azurite.

LEPIDOLITE

Freedom in relationships Make sure being lovestruck doesn't leave you feeling trapped by creating an "I'm fabulous" box and filling it with memories of fun times you've had without your partner. Look through it each night with a Lepidolite by your heart to ensure that "me" doesn't become "we."

Alternative gemstones
Rhodonite, Sunstone, Blue-Green Smithsonite.

Take a new relationship forward Turn Mr or Ms Possible into marriage material by wearing a Chrysanthemum Stone necklace on your next date, holding one close to your heart, or slipping one into your bra or pocket, to keep the attraction and passion between you sky-high.

CHRYSANTHEMUM STONE

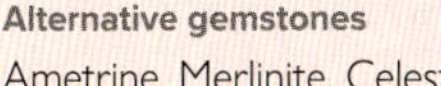

Alternative gemstones

Ametrine, Merlinite, Celestite.

A zest for romance According to legend, Saint Valentine (widely considered to be the patron saint of lovers) wore an Amethyst ring with an image of Cupid engraved on it. Wear one to inspire you to believe in love, just like he did, and remind you of the magic of being in love.

AMETHYST

Alternative gemstones

Cobaltoan Calcite, Pink Topaz, Pink Tourmaline.

Individuality in relationships If you have a soul (which I'm assuming you do, unless you're a vampire!) and are your own mate, guess what? You've already got a soulmate! Hold a Quantum Quattro to remind you of that, and ensure you turn the "w" in "we" upside down, and focus on "me" from time to time.

QUANTUM QUATTRO

Alternative gemstones

Chinese Chromium Quartz, Pyrophyllite, Candle Quartz.

CHALCEDONY

Meeting the in-laws Worried your in-laws will think you're a bore? Don't fret, simply add a Chalcedony to your evening ensemble to ensure they're super-impressed with your charisma and charm.

Alternative gemstones
Chrysoberyl, Spinel, Alexandrite.

DALMATIAN STONE

Wedding-day nerves Prevent nerves from spoiling your special day by rubbing a piece of Dalmatian Stone any time you start feeling stressed to keep any negative emotions in check.

Alternative gemstones
Watermelon Tourmaline, Abalone Shell, Amazonite.

Sexual connection According to Chinese legend, Yue Lao, a deity who sits under the Moon, ties an invisible red string between those who are destined to marry. Hang a Crystalline Kyanite on a red thread to help you and your partner feel more connected.

Alternative gemstones
Erythrite, African Jade, Rose Quartz.

CRYSTALLINE KYANITE

Trust in relationships The ancient Greeks and Romans believed Cupid's arrows were dipped in Diamonds before he fired them, giving them a power unlike any other. Wear one around your neck to ensure you believe in the arrows you catch.

DIAMOND

Alternative gemstones
Pink Agate, Rhodochrosite, Larimar.

Be an army of two A French fairy tale, *La Chatte Blanche* (The White Cat), tells the story of a prince who falls in love with a princess. But the princess has been turned into a cat by evil fairies. He breaks the spell by kissing her and they return to his father's castle wearing Rubies. Wear one to help you and your prince or princess unite against evil.

RUBY

Alternative gemstones
Diamond, Sardonyx, Green Sapphire.

Renewing love According to Inuit legend, there was once a reindeer girl called Tutu, who fled to the mountains to give birth to her first child. Her life-producing blood seeped into the stones, creating what we now call Tugtupite gemstones. Wear one to help you renew your love with your partner.

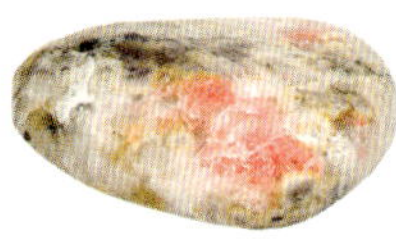
TUGTUPITE

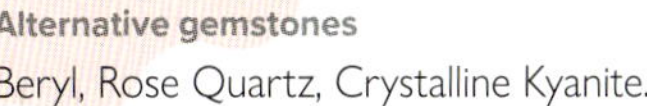

Alternative gemstones
Beryl, Rose Quartz, Crystalline Kyanite.

fear of heartbreak

Many people have real difficulty in allowing someone to get too close for fear of rejection and unbearable heartache. By not giving love a chance they miss so much that life has to offer. If you find yourself in this position, there are several things you can do.

First, banish any fears of rejection by holding a **Cassiterite** crystal to help you find the approval you seek within, and empower you to rely on yourself, rather than others, for acceptance. A **Rhodochrosite** pushed into the soil of a potted plant can encourage you to share your love with another. Visualize it helping your heart to unfurl like the petals of your beautiful flowers. Then a **Crystalline Kyanite** held by your heart will help you to overcome your hang-ups and embrace your date with destiny.

Remember that fortune favors the brave and no one deserves to be favored more than you. Make this your mantra by writing it down on a piece of paper and putting this in a pouch with an **Ajoite** to lessen your fear of giving your heart to another person.

CASSITERITE

RHODOCHROSITE

alternative gemstones

Cassiterite Strawberry Quartz, Lavender Pink Smithsonite, Pink Sapphire.

Rhodochrosite Pink Petalite, Pink Danburite, Mangano Calcite.

Crystalline Kyanite Green Tourmaline, Hemimorphite, Blue Lace Agate.

Ajoite Blue Quartz, Flint, Eudialyte.

CRYSTALLINE KYANITE

AJOITE

long-lasting love

GREEN JADE

Harmony in love Stay serene when your partner forgets to run errands or do chores by writing a list of everything you love about them, and reading through it with a Green Jade by your heart to prevent any little quirks from driving you crazy. It will keep the peace between you.

Alternative gemstones
Emerald, Rose Quartz, Fluorite.

ERYTHRITE

Nurturing love Roses are synonymous with romance. Treat yourself to a rosebush and pop an Erythrite in the soil to encourage the love between you and your partner to flower—like your lovely roses—and fill your life with beauty.

Alternative gemstones
Green Tourmaline, Yttrian Fluorite, Emerald.

EMERALD

Staying faithful In ancient times, people would keep Emeralds in their homes to encourage faithfulness in relationships. Place one in your bedroom to keep the flame of love between you and your partner burning brightly.

Alternative gemstones
Blue Tourmaline, Diamond, Chrysoprase.

Unconditional love "Even after all this time, the Sun never says to the Earth, 'you owe me.' Look what happens with a love like that, it lights the whole sky." The poet Hafiz beautifully described unconditional love in these lines. Place a Chrysoberyl somewhere visible to keep the love between you and your partner invincible.

CHRYSOBERYL

Alternative gemstones

Rose Quartz, Pink Danburite, Petalite.

Bonding with your partner Marriage isn't about falling in love with one person once, but falling in love with the same person every day. Keep an Ametrine in your bedroom to prevent the spark between you from fading away, and ensure you fall more in love with each other each day.

AMETRINE

Alternative gemstones

Celestite, Chrysanthemum Stone, Green Moss Agate.

Enduring love When it comes to love, you can't beat a dove! The birds are believed to mate for life, staying with the same partner forever. Place an image of a pair of turtledoves in your home, alongside a Lapis Lazuli, to inspire you and your partner to mate for life, too.

LAPIS LAZULI

Alternative gemstones

Green Sapphire, Diamond, Tugtupite.

work through issues

RHODONITE

Anger toward a partner Turn your relationship from testy to zesty by placing a Rhodonite crystal beside a photo of your partner to diffuse the tension between you, and ensure the only fireworks you create together are in the bedroom.

Alternative gemstones

Golden Calcite, Pink Carnelian, Lapis Lazuli.

SUGILITE

Envy in relationships According to an old Cherokee legend, we each have two wolves inside us, one called fear, the other named love. The wolf that comes out on top is the one we feed most. Wear a Sugilite necklace to prevent fear from outgrowing, or destroying, love in your relationship.

Alternative gemstones

Peridot, Rhodochrosite, Amethyst.

AFGHANITE

Arguments Disagreements are like a game of chess—they need two people to play. Walk away from them and no one can win. Wear an Afghanite ring on one of your fingers to prevent you from picking petty fights.

Alternative gemstones

Tugtupite, Limonite, Sugilite.

Feeling tied down The next time you start feeling overwhelmed, write an essential must-do list, and wear a Vera Cruz Amethyst necklace to help you distinguish between what's necessary (cooking dinner) and what's overgenerous (giving your partner a foot rub), and ensure you say "hell no" to the latter.

VERA CRUZ AMETHYST

Alternative gemstones

Shift Quartz, Tanzanite, Chrysoberyl.

Keep your spirits up When you're head over heels, but the object of your affections is playing it cool, play a defiant anthem and have yourself a singsong. Hold a Silver Leaf Jasper in one hand, a hairbrush in the other, and mime along in a mirror to feel better in no time.

SILVER LEAF JASPER

Alternative gemstones

Angel Aura Quartz, Chalcedony, Pink-Banded Agate.

Going through a rough patch A couple who had been married for 65 years said the secret to their long relationship was that they were from a time when you fixed something that was broken, rather than throwing it away. Hold a Black Moonstone to ensure you and your partner do the same, and find the strength to work through any difficult patches.

BLACK MOONSTONE

Alternative gemstones

Beryl, Larimar, Mangano Calcite.

SCHORL

Don't be influenced by negativity from others Our dating choices are just that—ours. Sometimes your friends might be surprised at your choice of partner. They might have your best interests at heart, but they could also be motivated by their own negativity or jealousy. Hold a Schorl to prevent other people's negativity from affecting your love life.

Alternative gemstones
Amber, Cassiterite, Diamond.

LAVENDER PINK SMITHSONITE

Guilt in relationships A relationship consumed by fear is likely to lead to stress. Banish any distrust between you and your partner by keeping a Lavender Pink Smithsonite in your bedroom.

Alternative gemstones
Rose Quartz, Peridot, Larimar.

Working through problems Relationships—like a story—are a work in progress. They're never finished, not really. They can always be rewritten, revised, and edited. Hold a Quantum Quattro to prevent the glitches in one chapter from making you write off your happy ever after.

Alternative gemstones
Eudialyte, Erythrite, Rose Quartz.

QUANTUM QUATTRO

Resentment in relationships People used to believe Topaz crystals produced their own light, and mariners would often use the gems to guide them when it was dark. Wear one to guide you and your partner through your sadness and help you find the light of your love when things feel dark.

BLUE TOPAZ

Alternative gemstones
Faden Quartz, Beryl, Opal.

Sexual droughts Rutilated Quartz is often referred to as Venus's Hair Stone, because it's thought to contain pieces of the love goddess's hair. Wear one around your neck the next time you and your partner go through a dry spell to help you get the chemistry back.

RUTILATED QUARTZ

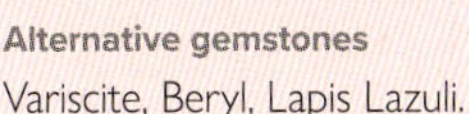

Alternative gemstones
Variscite, Beryl, Lapis Lazuli.

Toxic partners Some relationships are like mirrors—they help us to see ourselves in all our glory, but they are also fragile and easily broken. Hold a Rainbow Obsidian to prevent you from cutting yourself by trying to piece together something that can't be fixed.

Alternative gemstones
Obsidian, Aventurine, Peridot.

RAINBOW OBSIDIAN

passion and romance

RED GARNET

Keeping your partner interested A Red Garnet in the bedroom will reignite your partner's passion for you and yours for them. Your relationship will turn from fizzling to sizzling before you know it.

Alternative gemstones
Sardonyx, Emerald, Blue Sapphire.

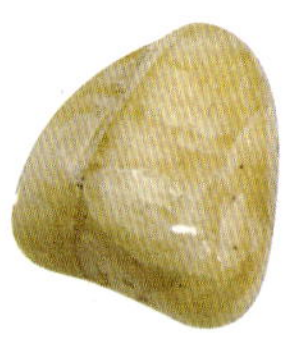
BERYL

Reinvigorate stale relationships Reignite the passion between you and your partner so it flares like a candle brightening up a dark room. Treat them to a candlelit meal, give Beryl as a gift, and keep one under your pillow to rekindle the flame between you.

Alternative gemstones
Morganite, Emerald, Diamond.

FALCON'S EYE

Spice up your relationship Swap mild and nice for hot and spicy by wearing a Falcon's Eye necklace to help you shed your inhibitions in bed, and ensure your clothes aren't the only things you throw off when the lights go off, but your insecurities, too.

Alternative gemstones
Gray-Banded Agate, Covellite, Quantum Quattro.

Rekindling love Reawaken the love between you and your partner by taking a fragranced bath together. Light a rose-scented candle and have some romantic music playing softly. A Lithium Quartz on the side will make all the difference.

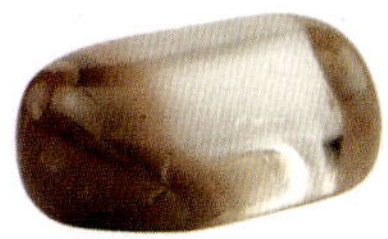

LITHIUM QUARTZ

Alternative gemstones
Vivianite, Beryl, Aegirine.

Sexual passion Swap sexual frustration for hot loving action by keeping a Red Jasper in your bedroom to help you shine like a star, and ensure things stay passionate between the sheets.

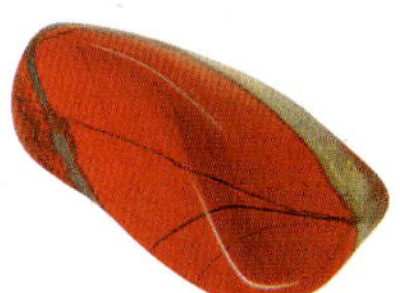

RED JASPER

Alternative gemstones
Red Garnet, Red-Black Obsidian, Poppy Jasper.

The art of seduction Embrace your inner sex kitten by placing a Ruby under your mattress to maximize your sexual confidence, and ensure you master the art of seduction to purr-fection!

RUBY

Alternative gemstones
Thulite, Garnet, Quantum Quattro.

breaking up

Everything ends. Endings are a part of life just as much as beginnings, and inevitably we have to learn to cope with them. Sometimes we don't know how strong we are until we're thrown into the ocean without a float, and realize we knew how to swim all along. Sometimes we have to fall apart, like beautiful but slightly cracked china, not because we're too weak to hold ourselves together, but because we're strong enough to know we can be better, and we deserve better.

A **Charoite** will help you to remember how well you were doing before your lost love affair, and to understand that you will love again, and a **Unakite** will ensure you carry on to become the best version of yourself you can be. An **Amblygonite** hung on a chain with a butterfly pendant will remind you that your heart's broken wings will soon mend.

As a form of therapy, start a "wisdom journal." Jot down anything you could have done differently, while holding a **Hawk's Eye**, to help you accept responsibility for your part in the relationship's breakdown. Then wash away any lingering sadness with an **Apache Tear** and use it to help you rise

UNAKITE

AMBLYGONITE

CHAROITE

from the ashes of heartache like a phoenix, feeling stronger, braver, and more emotionally liberated than ever.

alternative gemstones

Charoite Xenotime, Cobaltoan Calcite, Moss Agate.

Unakite Peach Selenite, Muscovite, Ethiopian Opal.

Amblygonite Moonstone, Peridot, Smoky Quartz.

Hawk's Eye Rhodonite, Rhodochrosite, Snow Quartz.

Apache Tear Mangano Calcite, Obsidian, Pink Sapphire.

HAWK'S EYE

APACHE TEAR

getting over heartbreak

FUCHSITE

Unrequited love Place a piece of Fuchsite by your heart to overcome the pain of unrequited love. The gem will soothe your sadness quicker than a box of your favorite chocolates, and help you remember what a catch you are.

Alternative gemstones

Chrysocolla, Rhodonite, Lavender Jade.

DIOPTASE

Betrayal Feeling more bitter than an artichoke? Give your heart an emotional overhaul by placing a Dioptase crystal over a photo of your ex. Spend five minutes sending them kind thoughts each night, and you'll soon notice your anger lessen.

Alternative gemstones

Amethyst, Agate, Pink Kunzite.

CROCOITE

Divorce Ease the pain of your divorce by wearing a Crocoite necklace to help you remember the good times you shared together, and empower you to see the lessons, and blessings, in your heartbreak.

Alternative gemstones

Melanite, Sulfur, Snowflake Obsidian.

Previous partners Most of us want to keep the ones who've hurt us as far away as possible, yet often bring them closer than ever by locking them in our hearts. Hold a Tugtupite over your heart to help you forgive the pain your ex has caused you, but never forget the lessons the relationship taught you.

TUGTUPITE

Alternative gemstones
Stibnite, Rhodonite, Rainbow Obsidian.

Healing a broken heart Hold an Elbaite over your heart, and imagine it putting the pieces back together, just like a stained glass window, and creating an even more magnificent whole from the broken fragments.

ELBAITE

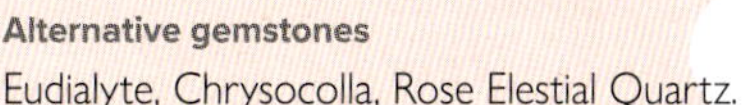

Alternative gemstones
Eudialyte, Chrysocolla, Rose Elestial Quartz.

Painful memories Reflecting on the past can bring such sweet sadness. We long for the times we were happiest, and rue the ones we were saddest. Hold a Strawberry Quartz by your heart to help you see the positive, however small, in your melancholy memories.

STRAWBERRY QUARTZ

Alternative gemstones
Cacoxenite, Stibnite, Goethite.

CHAROITE

Moving forward Swap past unhappiness for brighter tomorrows by writing a list of everything you'd like to release, and burning it with a candle flame. Bury the ashes in your garden, along with a Charoite crystal and some seeds, and both you and your plant will soon flourish.

Alternative gemstones
Gypsum, Chevron Amethyst, Dalmatian Stone.

HALITE

Don't be hung up on past loves They say every relationship teaches you something, so technically the more you have, the wiser you become! Affirm this to yourself any time you start missing an old lover, and hold a Halite to help you remember that sometimes new beginnings can only come from unhappy endings.

Alternative gemstones
Green Obsidian, Pink Petalite, Yellow Smithsonite.

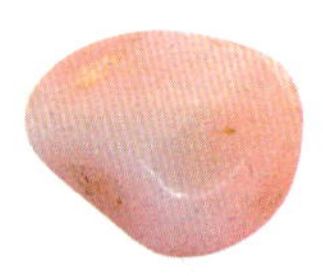
MANGANO CALCITE

Getting over the one who got away We all have someone who we can't quite seem to shake from our minds—a first love perhaps, or an ex-partner. Write that person a love letter while holding a Mangano Calcite, put it in an envelope with a few rose petals, and throw it into a lake or river to wash away your heart's ache.

Alternative gemstones
Orchid Calcite, Pink Petalite, Rainbow Obsidian.

Forgiveness Betrayal is the drop of ink that taints love's canvas; forgiveness is the water you throw on it to weaken its power. Hold a Rhodonite to help you forgive your partner's mistakes.

Alternative gemstones
Kutnohorite, Rhodochrosite, Chrysoberyl.

RHODONITE

Toxic exes Ex becoming a pest? Don't stress—hold a Pyrolusite by your chest! The gem's an absolute must for dealing with exes, and will prevent you from wasting time on Mr or Ms Wrong.

Alternative gemstones
Eudialyte, Amblygonite, Stibnite.

PYROLUSITE

Rebuilding trust According to ancient legends, Diopside was believed to have fallen from the tree of life, and is associated with renewal and rebirth. It is also thought to encourage emotional healing and growth, and is a wonderful crystal to turn to when you're seeking comfort during difficult times. Hold Diopside by your heart to help you to forgive a partner's dishonesty.

Alternative gemstones
Pink Topaz, Graphic Smoky Quartz, Pink Tourmaline.

DIOPSIDE

POWER CRYSTAL

rose quartz

Star signs Taurus, Libra
Planet Venus
Elements Earth, Water
Chakra Heart

Steeped in mystery and magic, Rose Quartz has long been highly prized for its powerful healing properties. Synonymous with unconditional love, joy, and healing, Rose Quartz is renowned for its naturally reassuring energy, which emanates from this beautiful pink crystal and encourages us to feel completely safe and at peace with ourselves. Rose Quartz promotes sensitivity, empathy, and compassion for ourselves and others. It's believed to bring happiness, romance, and beauty to anyone who beholds it, gently urging us to remember that we are worthy of love.

gem-scriptions

Attracting love Place a Rose Quartz under your pillow to draw your perfect partner into your life, and keep you looking radiant and youthful.
Relationships Display a few of the gems in each room to promote a loving, romantic atmosphere.
Self-love Wear a Rose Quartz necklace to bathe your heart in self-loving energy, and help you accept yourself wholeheartedly.

crystal cocktails

supercharge the gem's power

Rose Quartz + **Chrysocolla** = stabilize a rocky relationship

Rose Quartz + **Chyrosprase** = overcome jealousy

Rose Quartz + **Imperial Topaz** = improve self-confidence and become more extroverted

CHRYSOCOLLA

CHYROSPRASE

IMPERIAL TOPAZ

POWER CRYSTAL

ruby

Star signs Leo, Cancer, Scorpio, Sagittarius
Planet Mars
Element Fire
Chakra Heart

This stunning red stone represents devotion, desire, and passion, and is a symbol of eternal love. The Ruby is also associated with prediction and, in the Middle Ages, it was considered to be a stone of prophecy. In the sixteenth and seventeenth centuries, curative properties were also attributed to the stone. Wearing a striking piece of Ruby jewelry will bring good health, wisdom, and luck in love. It is a gem for true romantics and will help to fan the flames of desire in your relationship.

gem-scriptions

Spice up your relationship Wear a Ruby ring to increase the passion in your relationship and keep the flame of love alive.

Insightfulness If you're unsure whether or not to purse a new relationship, hold a Ruby while thinking about the new person in your life. The gem will enhance your intuition and you'll soon know if you've met Mr or Ms Right.

Moving on When you are struggling to get over a failed relationship, wear a Ruby over your heart to bring you healing and comfort, and attract new passions into your life.

crystal cocktails

supercharge the gem's power

Ruby + **Morganite** = improve your sex life

Ruby + **Fuchsite** = gain clarity if you are faced with a confusing love dilemma

Ruby + **Zoisite** = dissolve the painful feelings of unrequited love

MORGANITE

FUCHSITE

ZOISITE

CHAPTER TWO

home, family, and friendship

Heal rifts, strengthen bonds, and ensure your home is filled with happiness

happy household

SPIRIT QUARTZ

Communication at home Put a Spirit Quartz gemstone beside a photo of your family to spread a kind and loving energy through your abode, like a candle scenting the air, and to ensure everyone gets along.

Alternative gemstones

Jade, Rose Quartz, Moonstone.

BROWN TOURMALINE

Harmony at home Even the most saintly person gets annoyed sometimes. Place a Brown Tourmaline in your living room to avoid arguments with loved ones, and create a harmonious atmosphere.

Alternative gemstones

Spirit Quartz, Citrine, Chrysocolla.

PIETERSITE

Bring gratitude into your home "There are always flowers for those who want to see them"—artist Henri Matisse. Heed his advice by treating yourself to a bouquet of your favorite blooms each week, and placing a Pietersite by them to inspire you to see the roses rather than the thorns in every garden.

Alternative gemstones

Eilat Stone, Cavansite, Nebula Stone.

Build deeper bonds Place an Emerald crystal beside a photo of you and your loved ones and keep it in your living room to remind you of the happy times you've shared together, and help you see the best in each other.

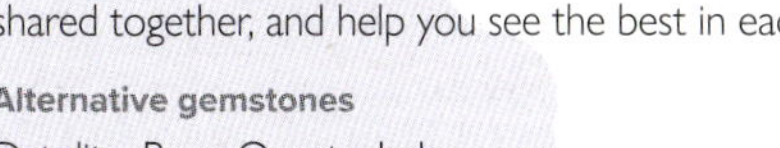

Alternative gemstones
Datolite, Rose Quartz, Jade.

EMERALD

Gratitude for loved ones Life can break our hearts, but the love we have for our family and friends reminds us how lucky we are. Fill a box with memories of times you've shared, and look at it while holding an Ocean Jasper by your heart to ensure you treasure the gems in your family jewelry box.

Alternative gemstones
Green Sapphire, Rose Quartz, Morganite.

OCEAN JASPER

Disorganization at home Keep a Marcasite crystal in your bedroom to improve your organizational skills, and make sure you don't leave the house without your keys and phone ever again!

Alternative gemstones
Hawk's Eye, Lapis Lazuli, Dumortierite.

MARCASITE

neighbors

In a busy world of work, family, and existing friends, it can be easy to forget that new friendship opportunities may present themselves right on your doorstep. Place a **Barite** by your door to inspire you to spread your social net, and when spending time with a neighbor, hold a **Blue Quartz**. This will ensure you don't overlook the gems in your neighborhood's treasure chest. Some people are like the crystals in this book—so small from afar, but more enchanting and powerful up close.

Of course, neighbors are not always a blessing. Some can be noisy, overly inquisitive, or downright unpleasant. The next time your new, music-loving neighbors start playing their favorite songs loudly, forget throwing a hissy fit. Simply hold a **Pyrite** to prevent you from taking life so seriously, and ensure they soon stop their raucousness. And when Mildred from next door starts poking about your business, give her the brush-off gem-style by placing a few **Agate** crystals by your front entrance. This will stop nosy neighbors from prying into your affairs.

They say revenge is a dish best served cold. Fiddlesticks! It's a dish guaranteed to leave you lying awake at night with "mood poisoning" until it's out of your system! Hold an **Ametrine** to help you overcome any

BARITE BLUE QUARTZ PYRITE

hostility toward your neighbors. In general, though, neighborhood drama is best avoided and you can protect your home's karma by placing a **Bloodstone** by your front door. This will prevent other people's wars from affecting you and yours, and ensure neighborhood gripes don't keep you up at night.

alternative gemstones

Barite Stone of Solidarity, Turquoise, Bowenite.

Blue Quartz Chrysopal, Flint, Sardonyx.

Pyrite Watermelon Tourmaline, Geothite, Pyromorphite.

Agate Hematite, Selenite, Obsidian.

Ametrine Fluorapatite, Aquamarine, Sugilite.

Bloodstone Cervantite, Agate, Amethyst.

AGATE

AMETRINE

BLOODSTONE

parenting

TIGER IRON

Tired parents Take a deep breath, close your eyes, and rub a Tiger Iron to help you cope with your kids' naughty antics, and prevent them from making you lose your temper.

Alternative gemstones
Mookaite, Pink Agate, Chrysoberyl.

CHALCEDONY

New mom Surf through your first birth by keeping a Chalcedony crystal by your heart to encourage your maternal instincts to kick in, and a bond to develop between you and your bundle of joy.

Alternative gemstones
Pink Agate, Rose Quartz, Mookaite.

RUBY

Stop your little ones from having bad dreams
Protect your children from nightly frights by slipping a Ruby under their pillows, or leave one by their window, to prevent bad dreams from keeping them awake.

Alternative gemstones
Pentagonite, Celestite, Flint.

Overcoming your parenting mistakes All parents make mistakes—even Buddha's father kept him locked away for years to protect him from the world's suffering, potentially denying us a whole faith—so, in the grander scheme of things, you're doing okay. Hold a Tangerine Quartz to ensure you know that.

TANGERINE QUARTZ

Alternative gemstones

Snowflake Obsidian, Chrysoprase, Rose Quartz.

Difficult teens Turn your troublesome teens into every parent's dream by slipping a Stichtite under their mattresses to prevent any door-slamming temper tantrums, and help them become delightful people.

STICHTITE

Alternative gemstones

Atlantasite, Stromatolite, Gray-Banded Agate.

Understanding your parents When our parents give us advice, it isn't because they did things perfectly every time, but because they made mistakes—and learned from them. Write down anything they tell you in a journal, and read through it while holding a Petalite, to ensure that you benefit from their wisdom.

PETALITE

Alternative gemstones

Ulexite, Barite, Cleavelandite.

family difficulties

BLUE AGATE

Arguments All families are slightly kooky, and those that aren't are even kookier for not being kooky. Learn to accept your relatives by placing a Blue Agate in your living room to avoid silly squabbles with loved ones.

Alternative gemstones
Diopside, Siberian Green Quartz, Green Agate.

BLUE MOONSTONE

Anger at home Stay zen when your family's driving you around the bend by placing a Blue Moonstone in your living room to improve relations between you, and prevent you from throwing a temper tantrum (or an apple pie!) at anyone.

Alternative gemstones
Spirit Quartz, Emerald, Agate.

RUTILATED QUARTZ

Meddling family Prevent your nosy family from driving you crazy by placing a Rutilated Quartz in a potted plant, and leaving it outside your front door to protect you from their meddling tomfoolery, and stop them from interfering in your life choices.

Alternative gemstones
Mookaite, Agate, Lavender Jade.

Say no to demanding relatives Hold a Brazilianite near your throat chakra to prevent you from caving in to others, despite any need to please. It will empower you to say no and stick to it the next time your sister-in-law asks for help with the garden pruning.

BRAZILIANITE

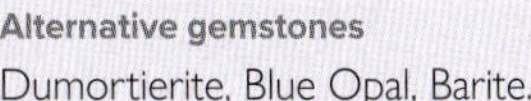

Alternative gemstones

Dumortierite, Blue Opal, Barite.

Sibling rivalry Replace your envious side with sibling pride by holding a Tourmalinated Quartz by your heart to help you rise above your jealousy, like a rainbow shining through the rain, knowing a pot of gold awaits you elsewhere.

TOURMALINATED QUARTZ

Alternative gemstones

Datolite, Blue Agate, Spirit Quartz.

Accepting change A great crystal to use when you're finding it difficult to accept the changes taking place in your life is Apatite. Hold one by your heart to help you welcome, rather than fight against, what's happening, and lessen your fear of the unknown.

APATITE

Alternative gemstones

Chrysocolla, Agate, Ajoite.

cleansing your home

A house full of negative energy can have an adverse effect on you and your family. Spritz each room with water in which a **Clear Quartz** has been left to soak in the sun for two hours to banish any harmful chi (energy). You could also hang some **Natural Quartz** crystals around your rooms, or dangle some from banisters or window frames to liven up the atmosphere.

A **Carnelian** outside your front door will protect you all from negativity. The gem will watch over your home, like a powerful sphinx, and placing an **Amethyst** indoors will perform the same function. Amethysts are said to have been created when the goddess Diana turned a young maiden, Amethystos, into the gemstone to protect her from the unwanted attentions of the god Dionysus. So Amethysts are great for all forms of protection.

CLEAR QUARTZ

NATURAL QUARTZ

alternative gemstones

Clear Quartz Smoky Rose Quartz, Malachite, Cavansite.

Natural Quartz Moonstone, Onyx, Malachite.

Carnelian Sulfur, Amethyst, Calcite.

Amethyst Fire Opal, Cobaltoan Calcite, Uvite Tourmaline on Magnesite.

CARNELIAN

AMETHYST

POWER CRYSTAL

emerald

Star signs Aries, Taurus, Gemini
Planet Venus
Element Earth
Chakra Heart

Known as "the stone of domestic bliss," this gem encourages us to remain rooted like a tree, to flower like a plant, and to give and receive nurture like everything in nature. These beautiful stones inspire us to love without condition, observe without judgment, and unite with those we cherish. If our relationships with our loved ones are the roses in our souls' gardens, Emeralds are the gardeners who water their soil. So whether you're seeking to sow seeds of forgiveness, water the "roses" in your family garden, or simply marvel at the beautiful flowers around you, this gem is the one to turn to.

gem-scriptions

Healing rifts Mend a broken relationship by writing a list of things you miss about your loved one, and sending it to them with an Emerald and a photo of the two of you together to renew the bond between you.

Deepening Pop an Emerald in a plant pot, and place it beside a family photograph to help nurture the love between you.

Appreciation Wear an Emerald necklace to ensure you tell those closest to you how much you love them.

crystal cocktails

supercharge the gem's power

Emerald + **Pink Crackle Quartz** = heal childhood wounds

Emerald + **Pink Agate** = deepen bond between parents and children

Emerald + **Spirit Quartz** = avoid petty arguments with loved ones

Emerald + **Stibnite** = prevent loved ones from snooping through your emails!

SPIRIT QUARTZ

POWER CRYSTAL

onyx

Star sign Leo
Planets Mars, Saturn
Element Earth
Chakra Root

Onyx is actually a type of Chalcedony and comes in a variety of colors. This grounding stone will promote happiness and stability at home and peaceful familial relations. Onyx is a wonderful stone to use if you need to let go of past hurts such as sibling rivalry or a difficult relationship with your parents. The stone has powerful protective qualities and is often used as a defense against negativity from other people. Onyx is also synonymous with self-mastery, inner strength, and resistance. It is a great gem to wear or carry when you need to bite your tongue or avoid lashing out!

gem-scriptions

Bring happiness into your home Place a pretty dish filled with Onyx in your hallway.

Deflect negative influences Slip a piece of Onyx into your child's schoolbag to keep them from falling in with the wrong crowd.

Keep calm during sibling arguments Hold an Onyx to diffuse the tension between you and your siblings.

crystal cocktails

supercharge the gem's power

Onyx + **Tiger's Eye** = stay grounded during stressful times

Onyx + **Agate** = create strong family bonds

Onyx + **Iolite** = protect your family from negative influences

TIGER'S EYE

AGATE

IOLITE

finding friends

SARDONYX

Attract new friends Draw people to you quicker than a bee to pollen by keeping a Sardonyx crystal in your bag, or placing one near your throat chakra. The crystal will get your social life buzzing in no time, and turn your home into a hive of activity.

Alternative gemstones

Turquoise, Danburite, Jade.

PETALITE

Don't be misled by false friends Place a Petalite under your pillow to help you find the answers you're seeking within yourself. The gem will empower you to follow, and trust, your own instincts and judgment, rather than relying on a friend who may turn out to be wrong for you.

Alternative gemstones

Phantom Quartz, Paraiba Tourmaline, Iceland Spar.

CHRYSOPRASE

Making new friends Feeling lonelier than a Fruit Loop in a bowl of Cheerios? Fear not, simply add a Chrysoprase to your party ensemble and rub it any time you start feeling anxious to maximize your personal charisma and help you make new friends.

Alternative gemstones

Ammolite, Chrysopal, Sardonyx.

Rekindling friendships True friends are like a good perfume or cologne—fabulous to go out with, great for your self-esteem, and something you feel incomplete without. Send an old friend a photo of the two of you together and a Nebula Stone, to remember the lovely times you shared and rediscover your friendship.

NEBULA STONE

Alternative gemstones

Diopside, Meteorite, Rose Quartz.

Stay true to your individuality Place a Bronzite crystal near a photo of someone you admire to inspire you to follow your own path in life, and become the person your younger self always hoped you'd be. Potential new friends will be attracted to your authenticity.

BRONZITE

Alternative gemstones

Carnelian, Diamond, Aegirine.

Attracting the right friends We're all a bit like crystals, each with our own properties that someone, somewhere is looking for. Hold a Zoisite by your heart to ensure you never hide your light but let it shine brightly. The perfect potential friends will be drawn to you, and everyone will accept you.

ZOISITE

Alternative gemstones

Coral, Green Tourmaline, Marcasite.

nurture your friendships

RED CALCITE

Entertaining friends Turn your social life from silent to vibrant by placing a Red Calcite in your dining room, and throwing a fabulous dinner party for your closest friends. This gem is thought to liven up any social gathering, and will ensure you're at the top of everyone's guest list.

Alternative gemstones
Pink Crackle Quartz, Turquoise, Danburite.

CHRYSOBERYL

Staying friends Diamonds might be a girl's best friend, but true friends are diamonds, too. Avoid fallouts by placing a Chrysoberyl beside a photo of you all together, and looking at it any time your friends annoy you to help you remember how special they are.

Alternative gemstones
Siberian Green Quartz, Green Agate, Smithsonite.

BARITE

Setting boundaries Self-care is an accessory nobody should be without. Complement yours with a Barite necklace to help you set healthier boundaries with others and ensure you, and they, don't overstep them.

Alternative gemstones
Lavender Jade, Brazilianite, Aventurine.

TANZINE AURA QUARTZ

Inspiring others Many of us wish we could go back in time and share the wisdom we now have with our younger selves. Be that person for someone else by wearing a Tanzine Aura Quartz by your heart to turn the weeds of your yesterdays into the seeds of others' brighter days.

Alternative gemstones
Tugtupite, Ocean Jasper, Lemurian Jade.

HELIODOR

Have compassion If our hearts are the Sun, our actions are the Moon that reflects its light. Hang a sun and moon pendant on a chain together with a Heliodor to inspire you to use your heart and mind to bring light into other people's darkest hours.

Alternative gemstones
Green Aventurine, Selenite, Spirit Quartz.

JADE

Saying thanks True friendships are like the branches of an ivy plant—they weave together, keep growing taller, and can withstand any weather. Send a Jade to your friends to let them know how happy you are to have them in your life.

Alternative gemstones
Barite, Turquoise, Watermelon Tourmaline.

forgiveness

Sometimes we need to forgive others, not because their actions were right, but to free ourselves from the burden of holding on to old grievances. To dissolve your anger and embrace forgiveness is incredibly empowering. If you can do it, you will feel emotionally fit and so much better.

Nelson Mandela once said, "As I walked toward the gate to my freedom, I knew if I didn't leave my bitterness and hate behind, I'd still be in prison." A piece of **Unakite** by your heart will help you to rid yourself of bitterness and forgive those who you feel have wronged you.

Let go of a grudge by holding an **Apache Tear** while writing a letter to the person who has caused these hard feelings. Then throw the letter into the ocean or a lake, knowing that such an action will bring you inner peace; or place it under a **Pink Calcite** and spend five minutes each night wishing your tormentor well. Your anger will soon lessen.

Buddha tells us that holding onto anger is like grasping a hot coal with the intent of throwing it at someone else—you're the one who gets burned. So Buddhists believe we aren't punished for our anger, but by it.

UNAKITE

APACHE TEAR

Make this your motto, and hold a **Diopside** to help you forgive those who've hurt you. If any regrets are holding you back, get rid of them, like a snake shedding its skin. An **Onyx** crystal over your heart will help, and will also promote forgiveness for the pain others have caused you.

alternative gemstones

Unakite Pink Calcite, Chrysoprase, Charoite.

Apache Tear Purple Moonstone, Sugilite, Chrysoberyl.

Pink Calcite Citrine, Chrysoprase, Sugilite.

Diopside Desert Rose, Brandberg Amethyst, Sugilite.

Onyx Snowflake Obsidian, Eudialyte, Greenlandite.

PINK CALCITE

DIOPSIDE

ONYX

friendship troubles

SMITHSONITE

Avoiding arguments As Gandhi once said, "An eye for an eye will only make the world blind." So why waste energy arguing with others, when you can spend it having a ball with them? Wear a Smithsonite necklace to avoid fallouts with friends and loved ones, and help you to see the best in everyone.

Alternative gemstones
Schalenblende, Green Garnet, Pietersite.

OCEAN JASPER

Unresolved issues Wash away past sorrows by writing a letter to the person who hurt you, and placing it under an Ocean Jasper overnight. Throw it into a lake or the ocean the following morning while holding your crystal, and watch it carry away your sadness.

Alternative gemstones
Petalite, Phantom Quartz, Dalmatian Stone.

FADEN QUARTZ

Achieve harmony in difficult friendships Struggling to see eye to eye with someone? Forget the drama, do the Metta Bhavana! This meditation is a fabulous stress buster, and works even better gem-style. Simply spend five minutes sending your friend love and kindness each day while holding a Faden Quartz to dissolve the tension.

Alternative gemstones
Peridot, Celestite, Siberian Green Quartz.

Avoid pessimistic people The next time someone starts raining on your parade, get out your umbrella and walk away. Simply wear a Black Obsidian to prevent other people's gloom from affecting your happiness.

BLACK OBSIDIAN

Alternative gemstones

Aventurine, Red Jasper, Ruby.

Backing down too often Sometimes you're given a really awful gift at Christmas, which you feel you have to accept gracefully. Petty squabbles with friends can be like that, but the longer you go on backing down gracefully, the more others will expect you to always accept their point of view. Wear an Atlantasite to help you break the pattern and stick to your own opinion when you know that you are in the right!

ATLANTASITE

Alternative gemstones

Amblygonite, Bornite, Bustamite.

Accepting you're wrong It's never easy to admit that you're in the wrong, but stubbornly refusing to back down in an argument could cost you a wonderful friendship. Hold a piece of Flint as you pick up the phone and call a friend to admit your mistake.

FLINT

Alternative gemstones

Dumortierite, Sulfur, Pietersite.

POWER CRYSTAL

jade

Star signs Aries, Taurus, Gemini, Libra
Planet Venus
Element Earth
Chakras Heart, Third Eye

Jade crystals have been synonymous with friendship for nearly 6,000 years, and feature in many of the world's greatest legends about selfless devotion to others. The physical strength, longevity, and priceless value of the gem itself beautifully encapsulates everything friendship entails. Jade encourages us to be virtuous, courageous, and uninfluenced by the actions of those whose values differ from our own.

gem-scriptions

New friends Treat yourself to a Jade necklace and wear it (along with a fabulous outfit and a smile) to the next party or social gathering you attend to attract new pals.

Broken friendships Send an old friend a bunch of yellow roses, which are linked with friendship, and slip a Jade into the card to heal your bond.

Deepening existing friendships Place a plant beside a photo of your closest friends, and pop a Jade in the soil to keep the connection between you strong.

crystal cocktails

supercharge the gem's power

Jade + **Sunstone** = help you to say no, and stand up for yourself

Jade + **Moss Agate** = turn a friendship into a relationship

Jade + **Carnelian** = remove jealousy between you and your friends

SUNSTONE

MOSS AGATE

CARNELIAN

POWER CRYSTAL

turquoise

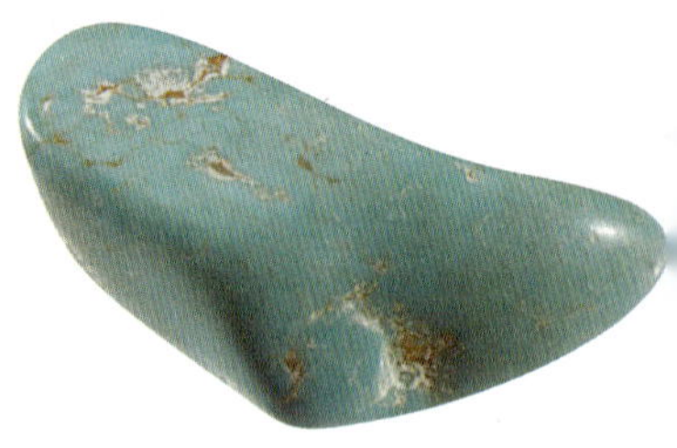

Star signs Sagittarius, Scorpio, Pisces
Planets Jupiter, Venus, Neptune
Elements Fire, Earth, Air
Chakras Throat, Third Eye

Strong yet soothing, Turquoise is a stone of protection and healing. This stunning blue gem was sacred to Hathor, the Egyptian goddess of joy and love, and also to the Aztecs and Native Americans. It is a stone of friendship and a perfect gift, as demonstrated by the Arabic proverb: "A Turquoise given by a loving hand carries with it happiness and good fortune." Working with Turquoise will bring peace to quarreling friends and good fortune to close friends.

gem-scriptions

Strengthen new friendships Give new friends a piece of Turquoise (perhaps a lovely piece of jewelry) to strengthen your bond and promote a long-lasting friendship.
Overcome shyness Wear a Turquoise necklace the next time you are going to meet new people to help you feel confident.
Appreciating your friends Meditate while holding a Turquoise and thinking about all the amazing friends in your life to help you truly appreciate their wonderful, unique qualities.

crystal cocktails

supercharge the gem's power

Turquoise + **Larimar** = bring healing to a damaged friendship

Turquoise + **Sodalite** = improve communication between friends

Turquoise + **Copper** = strengthen an existing friendship

LARIMAR

SODALITE

COPPER

CHAPTER THREE

work, career, and abundance

Impress your boss, boost your finances, and make crystal-clear decisions

in the workplace

BLUE KYANITE

Communicating with colleagues Place a Blue Kyanite on your desk to avoid silly squabbles with workmates, and prevent you from losing your temper the next time Mark from accounts starts hassling you again about when you're getting married, starting a family, or buying a home.

Alternative gemstones
Grossularite, Common Opal, Blue Moonstone.

COPPER

Impatience More restless than an espresso-loving woodpecker? Keep calm and carry a Copper! The gem will stop you from being so fidgety, and introduce you to someone you might not be familiar with—Master Patience, which is exactly what it will help you to do.

Alternative gemstones
Danburite, Watermelon Tourmaline, Emerald.

CHALCEDONY

Harmony at work Replace office rivalry with friendly camaraderie by treating your colleagues to a new indoor plant and slipping a Chalcedony behind it to help everyone get along better, and create a kind and loving atmosphere.

Alternative gemstones
Spirit Quartz, Yellow Fluorite, Sandstone.

Learning from others There are more than eight billion people in the world, and every single one of them knows something you don't. Start a wisdom journal, and write down anything enlightening that others tell you. Read through it while holding an Iceland Spar, to enrich your vision with their wisdom.

ICELAND SPAR

Alternative gemstones

Lepidolite, Galena, Hiddenite.

Achieve crystal-clear thinking Hold a White Calcite to your forehead any time your mind gets fuzzy. It's like having your very own internal housekeeper, and will ensure your inner world's as spick-and-span as your outer one.

WHITE CALCITE

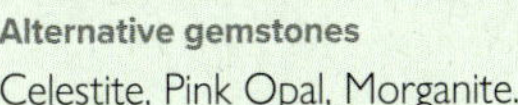

Alternative gemstones

Celestite, Pink Opal, Morganite.

Overcome ageism Success has nothing to do with age, so don't think that you won't get that promotion just because you're a bit older or younger than your colleagues. Wear Petrified Wood to ensure the lines on your face don't interfere with your pace in the workplace.

PETRIFIED WOOD

Alternative gemstones

Pink Crackle Quartz, White Opal, Youngite.

new job

Whether you're just starting out in the world of work or wanting to move on, a new job represents a radical change in your life and so is bound to get the nerves jangling. Calm pre-interview jitters by putting an **Amazonite** under your pillow to ensure you sleep well and are able to do yourself justice. For more of a helping hand, dress to impress by accessorizing your favorite lucky outfit with a **Hematite** crystal. The gem will strengthen your personal magnetism, and help you blow their

AMAZONITE

HEMATITE

SERPENTINE

socks off! Then, once you've been hired, waltz into your new job without any fear by carrying a **Serpentine** in your wallet or purse. This will help you to hit the professional ground running, and ensure you make a dazzling impression.

alternative gemstones

Amazonite Black Sapphire, Adamite, Magnetite.
Hematite Zircon, Mookaite, Carnelian.
Serpentine Yellow Tourmaline, Blue Sapphire, Cinnabar.

confidence is key

PERIDOT

Attract new clients Place a piece of Peridot in your purse or beside some money to wow potential business clients. It's believed to instantly boost your people power, and will magnify your natural charisma.

Alternative gemstones
Bowenite, Fire Opal, Carnelian.

HEMIMORPHITE

Completing projects Stick to your projects like icing on a cupcake by placing a Hemimorphite on your desk to help you stay motivated, and prevent you from giving up before the recipe for your success is fully baked and served to perfection.

Alternative gemstones
Honey Calcite, Picasso Marble, Red Chalcedony.

AFRICAN JADE

Selling skills Amaze prospective buyers with your magical ability to sell and make sure they fall under your spell by wearing an African Jade necklace to maximize your natural charm, and make you luckier than a four-leaf clover.

Alternative gemstones
Cinnabar, Thulite, Golden Topaz.

Uncertainty at work Hold a Tanzanite by your heart to clear away any clouds, such as other people's opinions, which may be preventing you from sharing your gifts with the world. It will free your talent to shine through, like the Sun, and help you see your destiny.

TANZANITE

Alternative gemstones
Stibnite, Lodestone, Sugilite.

Express your talents As spiritual teacher and writer Marianne Williamson once said, "There's nothing enlightened about shrinking so others won't feel insecure around you." Shine bright, like a Diamond, by wearing one around your neck to inspire you to share your light with the world.

DIAMOND

Alternative gemstones
Astrophyllite, Yellow Topaz, Marcasite.

Witty response The next time your boss puts you on the spot, dazzle them with your humor and razor-sharp wit by keeping a Watermelon Tourmaline in your pocket to help your confidence soar sky-high.

Alternative gemstones
Goethite, Pyromorphite, Snakeskin Agate.

WATERMELON TOURMALINE

lack of confidence

Everyone knows that self-doubt is an obstacle to be overcome on the way to success, but that doesn't mean that confidence comes easily, although it can easily take a knock. When your faith in yourself needs a boost, wear a piece of **Golden Calcite** around your neck to help you see how gifted and worthy of success you are, and remember the words of former First Lady Eleanor Roosevelt—"No one can make you feel inferior without your consent." Wearing a **Stichtite** and **Serpentine** will help to boost your self-perception, and remind you that you are just as good as anyone else.

The only difference between victim and victor is perception. As Buddha said, "what you think, you become," so, in other words, to be a champion you must think like one. Put your victim mentality to rest by holding a **Realgar** and **Orpiment** by your chest; and should the occasion arise when you've just got to be so utterly fabulous that no one can knock you, hold an **Epidote in Quartz**, affirm that you are utterly fabulous, and kick out any mental block that's stopping you from forging ahead.

SERPENTINE

REALGAR

GOLDEN CALCITE

STICHTITE

alternative gemstones

Golden Calcite Chrysoberyl, Mangano Calcite, Pink Kunzite.

Stichtite and Serpentine Yellow Jasper, Garnet, Lavender Pink Smithsonite.

Realgar and Orpiment Lapis Lazuli, Tourmaline, Snow Quartz.

Epidote in Quartz Quantum Quattro, Smithsonite, Angelite.

ORPIMENT

EPIDOTE IN QUARTZ

making progress

JASPER

Taking action There's only one place where progress comes before work and that's in the dictionary! So stop dreaming and start scheming by placing a Jasper crystal in your office to help you get your projects out of your head, and into the world.

Alternative gemstones
Septarian, Diamond, Tiger's Eye.

TIGER'S EYE

Deal with holding-back syndrome There are between 25,000 and 30,000 days in the average lifetime and "someday" isn't one of them, so stop waiting and start creating by placing a Tiger's Eye over your bucket list to help you seize the day—today!

Alternative gemstones
Sardonyx, Red Calcite, Golden Topaz.

METAMORPHOSIS QUARTZ

Go your own way To paraphrase playwright George Bernard Shaw: life isn't about finding yourself, but creating your (best) self. Follow his advice by wearing a Metamorphosis Quartz around your neck to help you shape your own destiny, find your ideal career, and write the perfect ending to your handmade fairy tale.

Alternative gemstones
Goshenite, Shattuckite, Blue Sapphire.

Changing direction A man walked down a road and straight into a puddle. The next day, he took the same road, walked around the puddle, but stumbled and stepped in. On the third day, he took a different road. Hold a Stichtite to prevent you from walking into the same puddles time and time again.

STICHTITE

Alternative gemstones

Chrysoberyl, Charoite, Moonstone.

Believe there are no ill winds We all make mistakes and an Onyx will help to you see that every cloud has a silver lining. Hold one of these beautiful stones to help you see the upside of your mistakes.

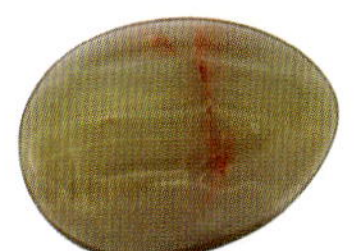

ONYX

Alternative gemstones

Snowflake Obsidian, Eudialyte, Wind Fossil Agate.

Be ambitious Helen Keller, deafblind author, political activist, and lecturer, once said, "The only thing worse than being blind is having sight but no vision." Place a Vivianite over your eyes to help you heed her wisdom and prevent you from limiting your ambition.

VIVIANITE

Alternative gemstones

Jade, Leopardskin Jasper, Idocrase.

having a bad day

SMOKY QUARTZ

Anger at work Avoid petty fallouts with colleagues by keeping a Smoky Quartz on your desk. The gem will surround you in a bubble of positive energy, and help you focus on what you, rather than Janice in IT, should or shouldn't be doing.

Alternative gemstones
Bloodstone, Sugilite, Blue Kyanite.

HALITE

Dealing with setbacks at work Marilyn Monroe was once told she had no future in showbusiness. Did she give up? Hell, no! Handle any rejections Marilyn-style by wearing a pendant with the word "dream" and a Halite around your neck to prevent you from giving up on yours, however much you're tested.

Alternative gemstones
Cleavelandite, Cassiterite, Cobaltoan Calcite.

MERLINITE

Professional guilt We all want to be super-successful, and that can mean sacrificing parts of our personal lives for our professional ones. Make sure you get the balance right by placing a Merlinite under your pillow to help you find the perfect way to dance your way to the top.

Alternative gemstones
Ulexite, Zircon, Mookaite.

Overcome indecisiveness Hold an Azurite crystal to help you view your choices more objectively, and give you the courage to trust your own judgment.

Alternative gemstones
Rutilated Quartz, Green Tourmaline, Ruby.

AZURITE

Criticism We all love gifts, and the more we're given, the greater the chances we'll find something we can use. It's the same with criticism, which doesn't have to be negative. Write down any criticism you receive and hold a Kunzite to help you read between the lines and see the gifts in what you find.

Alternative gemstones
Sunstone, Fire Opal, Cassiterite.

KUNZITE

Office politics They say money's the root of all evil, and when people are competing for a promotion, or trying to impress the boss, office life can become tense and stressful. Place a Schalenblende beside a vase of white tulips (which represent forgiveness and fresh starts) in your office to weed out any rivalry and restore harmony.

Alternative gemstones
Flint, Grossularite, Calcite Fairy Stone.

SCHALENBLENDE

speaking to a crowd

Many people find speaking in public daunting, whether it be in meetings or a presentation to a larger audience. If you're required to make a speech, and it's causing you grief, keep a **Blue Apatite** with you for a few days and spend 15 minutes each night practicing what you're going to say. Imagine yourself receiving lots of applause, then slip into bed, confident that all will be well.

Words are powerful, but sometimes at work our voices are drowned out by louder colleagues. If having your say at meetings is a challenge, due to more forceful speakers or your lack of confidence, do a mini-visualization beforehand. Simply hold a **Green Agate** and imagine yourself performing brilliantly. Take the gem into the meeting with you, and smile as you make your points. Wearing a **Bronzite** will help you make yourself heard and allow you to shine.

alternative gemstones

Blue Apatite Blue Crackle Quartz, Blue Kyanite, Turquoise.

Green Agate Sodalite, Amethyst, Celestite.

Bronzite Dendritic Chalcedony, Stromatolite, Purpurite.

BLUE APATITE

GREEN AGATE

BRONZITE

dealing with negativity

There's nothing more annoying than someone saying you can't do something, and nothing more gratifying than listening to what they say and doing it anyway! Holding a Tree Agate will prevent other people's negativity from bringing you down. Alternatively, pop on your headphones, hold an Aqua Aura, and play your favorite happy song. It will drown out their negativity (literally!), and ensure you keep dancing on the inside, no matter what's happening around you.

alternative gemstones

Tree Agate Rutilated Kunzite, Trummer Jasper, Silver Leaf Jasper.
Aqua Aura Blue Tourmaline, Aventurine, Diamond.

TREE AGATE

AQUA AURA

financial success

TREE AGATE

Improve your finances Nurture your finances by putting a Tree Agate in a flowerpot with your favorite plant. The gem will maximize your cash flow, and ensure your bank balance and plant continue to blossom.

Alternative gemstones
Epidote, Emerald, Green Moss Agate.

CINNABAR

Creating abundance Become your own money-making genie by placing a piece of Cinnabar in your savings box to multiply your existing income, and guarantee you're never short of cash-raising ideas.

Alternative gemstone
Malachite, Green Tourmaline, Tiger's Eye.

Change your luck Stop feeling unlucky and start earning lots of money by slipping an Adamite in your mailbox to help you climb the professional ladder with amazing speed and dexterity.

Alternative gemstones
Cinnabar, Black Sapphire, Serpentine.

ADAMITE

Anxiety about money A brilliant stone to use when you're feeling anxious about your finances is Jade. Place it by your heart to overcome any negative beliefs or self-destructive patterns that may be affecting your relationship with money.

JADE

Alternative gemstones

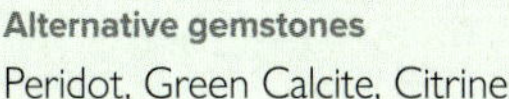

Peridot, Green Calcite, Citrine.

Avoid overspending An absolute must for shopaholics is Vanadinite. Take one on your next shopping spree to prevent any excessive splash-outs.

VANADINITE

Alternative gemstones

Smoky Quartz, Green Quartz, Green Spinel.

Attracting abundance Keep a Citrine gemstone in your purse, wallet, or beside some money to increase your financial success. It will boost your money-making mojo, and turn you into an instant cash magnet.

CITRINE

Alternative gemstones

Jade, Jet, Yellow Sapphire.

POWER CRYSTAL

tiger's eye

Star signs Leo, Capricorn
Planet Sun
Elements Fire, Earth
Chakras Solar Plexus, Third Eye

A stone of integrity, confidence, and courage, Tiger's Eye empowers us to walk away from the handmade cage of self-doubt we've built for ourselves, and fulfill our true potential. It encourages us to explore our hidden talents and learn how to live by our own rules. Synonymous with career success, Tiger's Eye inspires us to focus on our prey, form a strategy for attack, and pounce when the moment's right. This gem discourages power struggles of all kinds but pushes us to soar, knowing that the "power" we allow others simply gives us more.

gem-scriptions

Daily tasks Place a Tiger's Eye over a list of your tasks for the day, and rub it any time your motivation wanes to boost your willpower.
Dreams Create a vision board of all the things you'd like to do, and spend five minutes looking at it each day while holding a Tiger's Eye to inspire you to make your dreams a reality.
Power struggles Keep a Tiger's Eye crystal on your desk to avoid power struggles with colleagues.

crystal cocktails

supercharge the gem's power

Tiger's Eye + **Citrine** = remove fear of responsibility

Tiger's Eye + **Blue Lace Agate** = help you express your ideas

Tiger's Eye + **Agate** = find courage to start again

CITRINE

BLUE LACE AGATE

AGATE

POWER CRYSTAL

jasper

Star sign Leo
Planets Sun, Mars
Element Fire
Chakra Root

Mysterious and captivating, Jasper is famous for its ability to protect and instill confidence and courage in its owner and it has long been considered a sacred and powerful stone. It acts as a professional support for those in jobs requiring strength and stamina, such as police officers. This crystal also brings energy and alertness to workers who must focus intensely on the task at hand, such as doctors. Wearing a piece of Jasper jewelry will help you to keep calm during stressful times at work, and it will also promote harmony among you and your colleagues. Use this balancing stone to help you achieve your career goals and be successful, whatever your job.

gem-scriptions

Give confident presentations Overcome nerves about public speaking by wearing an item of Jasper jewelry on the day of your presentation.
Stop procrastinating Keep a piece of Jasper on your desk to ensure you stay focused and work through your to-do list in super-quick time.
Deal with negative colleagues Hold a piece of Jasper when speaking to a grumpy colleague to prevent their negativity from affecting your mood.

crystal cocktails

supercharge the gem's power

Jasper + **Amethyst** = create positive energy in the workplace

Jasper + **Lepidolite** = banish work stress

Jasper + **Merlinite** = find the perfect work-life balance

AMETHYST

LEPIDOLITE

MERLINITE

POWER CRYSTAL

citrine

Star signs Aries, Gemini, Leo, Libra
Planets Sun, Jupiter
Element Air
Chakra Solar Plexus

Citrine crystals are the working-class heroes of the gem world. Associated with prosperity and wealth, the stone is actually one of the least expensive to buy. It encourages us to aim for the big things, and appreciate the small ones while inspiring us to invest in our greatest asset—our minds—with confidence and self-belief, ensuring any negative savings we've accumulated, such as self-doubt and fear, are swiftly dispersed. Citrine is a teacher, motivator, and life coach, supporting us through any doubts about our worth by reminding us what we deserve—we can't win the lottery without buying a ticket, get our dream job without applying for it, or reach the top of the ladder if we haven't stepped on it.

gem-scriptions

Attract cash Place Citrine crystals around your living room to ensure more money comes your way—and fast.
Sell your home Place a few Citrine stones around your home to maximize your property's appeal.
Increase your takings Put a Citrine gemstone in your takings box or till to attract lots of new customers.

crystal cocktails

supercharge the gem's power

Citrine + **Smoky Quartz** = prevent overspending

Citrine + **Morganite** = attract love

Citrine + **Emerald** = heal family rifts

SMOKY QUARTZ

MORGANITE

EMERALD

CHAPTER FOUR

health and well-being

Develop intuition, overcome self-doubt, and unlock your creativity

body beautiful

ROSE QUARTZ

Complexion perfection Boost your complexion by placing a Rose Quartz crystal in your bathwater. It's like all your favorite pampering essentials combined in a gemstone, and will leave you looking and feeling wonderful.

Alternative gemstones
Jade, Tanzanite, Almandine Garnet.

SNOWFLAKE OBSIDIAN

Detoxing Start your purifying regime by keeping a Snowflake Obsidian by your fridge to help you make wiser food choices, and prevent you from raiding the cookie jar!

Alternative gemstones
Pink-Banded Agate, Ruby, Chlorite.

AMBER

Enhancing beauty Rub a piece of Amber on your skin to bring out your natural beauty. It's an absolute must for nights out with friends, and will turn you into an instant object of desire.

Alternative gemstones
Aquamarine, Spinel, Imperial Topaz.

Wrinkle-busting Feeling wrinklier than a prune? Defy the laws of aging by placing an Opal crystal in your tub to improve your skin's elasticity, and leave you looking as smooth as a fresh plum.

Alternative gemstones
Sapphire, Moonstone, Pearl.

OPAL

Be body confident Boost your body image by placing a Magnesite crystal and a notebook on your bedside table. Write down five things you like about yourself each morning, and keep the gem and journal with you all day. Your confidence will soon skyrocket!

Alternative gemstones
Vanadinite, Chrysoprase, Rhodochrosite.

MAGNESITE

Weight loss A brilliant crystal to use when you're hoping to lose weight is Mookaite. Place one by your secret snacking stash to avoid any late-night chocolate binges.

Alternative gemstones
Unakite, Seraphinite, Quartz.

MOOKAITE

emotional healing

VERDELITE

Accepting your feelings Our emotions can be like the ocean—reflecting the Sun's light during our soul's summer, and absorbing the world's tears when the heavens open. Hang a Verdelite on a yin-yang necklace to help you accept the natural tides of your mind.

Alternative gemstones
Gray-Banded Agate, Pumice, Brazilianite.

CHRYSOBERYL

Heal your heart Wear the ultimate heart healer, Chrysoberyl, around your neck to overcome any toxic thinking patterns that are causing you pain.

Alternative gemstones
Larimar, Pink Tourmaline, Hemimorphite.

LARIMAR

Overcoming fear Awaken the hero within by holding a Larimar crystal whenever you're feeling anxious about something in particular. It will help give you the courage to embrace what you're afraid of, and empower you to feel the fear and do it anyway!

Alternative gemstones
Citrine, Charoite, Hematite.

Harness protective energy Be moved by the world without being broken by it—like a tree swaying in the wind—by sitting with your back against a tree while holding a Magnetite to prevent other people's sorrow from leaving you feeling empty.

MAGNETITE

Alternative gemstones

Kunzite, Ruby, Aventurine.

Removing blocks to healing As writer Haruki Murakami once said, "Pain is inevitable. Suffering is optional." Hold an Okenite by your heart, or wear one around your neck, to ensure you're the healer of your sadness, rather than the one encouraging it to linger.

OKENITE

Alternative gemstones

Morganite, Mangano Calcite, Blue Obsidian.

Don't be in denial Buddha was a prince who had been protected from the world's suffering. One day he ventured into the streets and was shocked to discover that everyone, including him, would die. Hold a Vivianite to prevent you from closing your mind to the truths you are trying to ignore.

VIVIANITE

Alternative gemstones

Porphyrite, Rhodochrosite, Morganite.

satisfaction

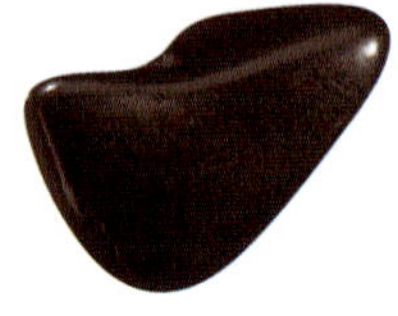
JET

Contentment Keep a Jet crystal in your pocket to help remind you of all that you've achieved and how far you've come. The gem's thought to keep you feeling happy, calm, and grounded, and will help you feel blessed, rather than stressed, all day, every day.

Alternative gemstones
Peridot, Pyrite, Jade.

RAINBOW OBSIDIAN

Count your blessings Adopt a *la vie en rose* (French for "life in pink") view of the world by wearing a Rainbow Obsidian around your neck to help you see and appreciate the beauty in everything, however challenging.

Alternative gemstones
Sapphire, Turquoise, Tree Agate.

BLUE TOPAZ

Cultivate enthusiasm The word "enthusiasm" comes from the Greek term *enthousiasmos*, meaning the "God within." Hold a Blue Topaz by your heart to inspire you to follow your dreams and embrace your destiny.

Alternative gemstones
Bustamite, Yellow Topaz, Aegirine.

Rebuilding happiness As poet, writer, and philosopher Ralph Waldo Emerson said, "Happiness is a perfume you can't pour on others without getting on yourself." Heed his words by doing a random act of kindness every day for a week, and holding a list of your deeds and a Sapphire any time your sparkle fades.

SAPPHIRE

Alternative gemstones

Cobaltoan Calcite, Turquoise, Tree Agate.

Gratitude for the self Turn your inner critic into a fan by holding an Almandine Garnet, and adding 15 minutes of "me time" to your day. The gem will encourage you to be kinder to yourself, and empower you to nurture, rather than torture, your soul's rapture.

ALMANDINE GARNET

Alternative gemstones

Pink Crackle Quartz, Pink Danburite, Strawberry Quartz.

Gratitude for the past Right now, you're wiser than you've ever been. Celebrate this by writing your sorrows on a piece of paper, and the lessons they taught you on another. Burn the first while holding a Goethite and watch as your past burns to oblivion, leaving you with only its wisdom.

GOETHITE

Alternative gemstones

Wind Fossil Agate, Cleavelandite, Creedite.

dreams

We all dream but remembering them is another matter. Wouldn't it be wonderful if we could experience fully, and savor, each and every moment of our lifetime, whether waking or sleeping? However, that requires us not only to remember our dreams but to understand and interpret them, too—all a bit of a tall order, but, as ever, crystals can help.

A **Prehnite** placed over your third eye chakra before bedtime will help you recall everything from your nightly escapades, aided by a **Malachite** in a pouch under your pillow. Keep a pen and notebook by your bed, and write down everything you remember in the morning. Repeat the process each day, and you'll soon realize what your heart is telling you. In the same way that everyone we meet teaches us something, many dreams bring messages and can provide answers if we are seeking guidance. Keep a **Boulder Opal** under your pillow, and record everything you remember to help you unravel the riddles in your nighttime wanderings, or a **Molybdenite** to come up with the advice you need.

Of course, not all dreams are good ones and no one wants to encourage nightmares. A **Celestite** crystal on your bedside table has the effect of an angel watching over you while you sleep. If a bad dream does manage to creep

PREHNITE MALACHITE BOULDER OPAL

LEPIDOLITE

through, try this super-simple pick-me-up ritual in the morning. Place a **Lepidolite** in your bathroom, jump in the shower, and imagine the water washing away the night's terror. You'll soon feel peachy again. Avoidance is better than cure, though, so to dispense with nighttime terrors and turn yourself into a keen, serene dreaming machine, keep a **Green Opal** crystal with you all day. It'll awaken (pun intended!) your imagination, and make sure your sleeping world is as fabulous as your waking one.

alternative gemstones

Prehnite Red Jasper, Mookaite, Poppy Jasper.
Malachite Larvikite, Kyanite, Smoky Quartz.
Boulder Opal Andalusite, Picasso Marble, Fluorite.
Molybdenite Shaman Quartz, Adamite, Fenster Quartz.
Celestite Gold, Ruby, Mangano Calcite.
Lepidolite Clinohumite, Copper, Peridot.
Green Opal Jade, Moldavite, Spirit Quartz.

MOLYBDENITE

CELESTITE

GREEN OPAL

be the best version of you

SUNSTONE

Expressing yourself Many of us hide our true selves from the world, never knowing who could be longing to meet the person we've locked away. Do them, and yourself, justice by wearing a Sunstone necklace to empower you to reveal your inner beauty to others.

Alternative gemstones
Variscite, Howlite, Jade.

ZOISITE

Embrace your kookiness The philosopher Nietzsche once said, "Those who danced were thought to be quite mad by those who couldn't hear the music." Be your own kind of kooky fabulous by hanging a Zoisite on your brightest necklace to lessen your fear of ridicule.

Alternative gemstones
Aegirine, Blue Lace Agate, Charoite.

BOULDER OPAL

Personal growth Growing older might be inevitable, but growing up is definitely optional! Make sure your inner and outer worlds stay in sync by starting a diary. Every evening, hold a Boulder Opal and jot down everything you've learned that day to help you become wiser with age.

Alternative gemstones
Tourmaline, Amazonite, Aquamarine.

The power of imagination A life without imagination is like a world without birdsong—still beautiful, but not quite as wonderful. Place an Ulexite under your pillow to keep yours strong. Then wherever you are, and whatever you're going through, your life will always be full of song.

Alternative gemstones
Diamond, Rose Quartz, Opal.

ULEXITE

Staying positive Place a Tangerine Quartz by your heart any time your hope waivers to help you see the good in every goodbye, the ray of sunshine in every betrayal, and the trophy in every catastrophe.

Alternative gemstones
Anhydrite, Azeztulite, Stibnite.

TANGERINE QUARTZ

Sharing hope As Buddha said, "Thousands of candles can be lit from a single candle and the life of the candle will not be shortened." Happiness never decreases by being shared, and hope is the same. Send a White Calcite to someone who's lost their hope to relight it with yours.

Alternative gemstones
Mangano Calcite, Lepidocrocite, Blue Quartz.

WHITE CALCITE

PYROMORPHITE

Humor A laugh a day keeps the blues away. Affirm this to yourself whenever life gets too serious. Look in a mirror, hold a Pyromorphite on your forehead, and pull the silliest face you can. You'll soon feel chirpier.

Alternative gemstones
Goethite, Watermelon Tourmaline, Pink Crackle Quartz.

VARISCITE

Staying strong Hope is the little voice telling you to "keep trying" when your faith is waning. Wear a Variscite to strengthen your belief in brighter tomorrows, and to help you stay strong till the end of your troubles.

Alternative gemstones
Moss Agate, Pietersite, Spectrolite.

VIVIANITE

Following your intuition Turn your inner knowledge into a source of courage by holding a Vivianite on your third eye chakra to incite your intuition to awaken, and help you find the salvation you seek within.

Alternative gemstones
Rutile, Tiffany Stone, Annabergite.

Authenticity "In order to be irreplaceable one must always be different." Channel Coco Chanel's wisdom by wearing an Indicolite to inspire you to be your own kind of beautiful, and the best and most authentic you possible.

INDICOLITE

Alternative gemstones
Goshenite, Bronzite, Turquoise.

Be realistic Willow trees are thought to have originally stood upright, but were so saddened by the world's plight, they bent over in sadness, vowing to stand straight only when happiness came to all. Wear a Scapolite to prevent you from punishing yourself for what couldn't be helped.

SCAPOLITE

Alternative gemstones
Agrellite, Larimar, Tourmalinated Quartz.

Be imaginative Ancient Persians used to believe the world was seated on a giant Blue Sapphire, which painted the sky blue, and reflected the color of heaven. Wear one to inspire you to see the world as colorfully as they did.

BLUE SAPPHIRE

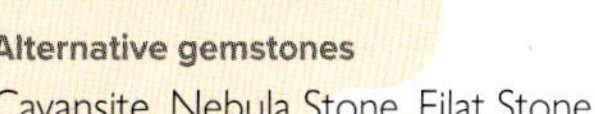

Alternative gemstones
Cavansite, Nebula Stone, Eilat Stone.

overcoming injustice

There was once a Welsh goddess, Rhiannon, who was falsely accused of murdering her son, and punished by her kingdom. She accepted her fate with dignity, and was eventually exonerated and reunited with her child, who had been kidnapped. Feeling anger at injustice is natural, so accepting the situation is not easy. A **Tugtupite** by your heart or around your neck will prevent your anger from harming you further, while a **Fire Opal**, symbolizing Rhiannon's virtuous qualities, will help you to forgive those who have wronged you, as she did.

If you need to take more action to help you deal with your sense of unfairness, write the word "injustice" down the edge of a page and then one thing you've learned from the experience next to each letter. Make it rhyme if you can, and read through it with a **Boji Stone** by your heart to help you see the blessings in your heartache.

TUGTUPITE

FIRE OPAL

Otherwise, place a **Lemon Chrysoprase** in a musical jewelry box, and spend five minutes each night watching the ballerina dancing around to remind you that what goes around comes around, and that in time karma will prevail.

alternative gemstones

Tugtupite Citrine Spirit Quartz, Peach Selenite, Amethyst.

Fire Opal Prehnite, Sugilite, Chrysoberyl.

Boji Stone Fire Opal, Watermelon Tourmaline, Actinolite.

Lemon Chrysoprase Rhodonite, Limonite, Variscite.

BOJI STONE

LEMON CHRYSOPRASE

facing obstacles

AMETHYST

Insomnia Swap counting sheep for blissful sleep by creating your own dream pillow. Pop some dried lavender buds and an Amethyst on to a piece of fabric, tie it together, and place it under your pillow. Then snuggle into bed, shut your eyes, and say goodbye to sleepless nights forever.

Alternative gemstones
Hematite, Chrysoprase, Lapis Lazuli.

ALEXANDRITE

Breaking bad habits Give your willpower a boost by writing a list of five reasons why you'd be happier, healthier, and better off without your habit, and placing it under an Alexandrite. Look at it any time your determination wanes to help you stay strong.

Alternative gemstones
Ruby, Peridot, Black Onyx.

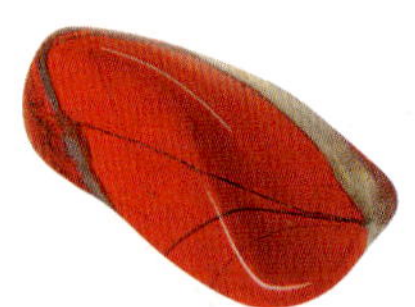
RED JASPER

Fresh starts Hold a Red Jasper gemstone to help you emerge from any difficulty, like a caterpillar leaving its cocoon to become a butterfly, ready to spread your wings, and start a new phase in your life.

Alternative gemstones
Spinel, Charoite, Chiastolite.

Aimlessness Feeling a little lost? Every evening, take a 15-minute walk, carrying a Lapis Lazuli with you, and think about five good things that happened in your day. Repeat the ritual every evening, and keep the gem with you all day. You'll soon know where your heart lies.

LAPIS LAZULI

Alternative gemstones

Barite, Thulite, Titanium Quartz.

Self-judgment Judgment loves company and rarely comes to us alone. We judge others for not living up to our expectations, then judge ourselves for misjudging them. Place an Ajoite by your heart to help you forgive your past errors.

AJOITE

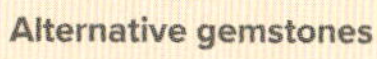

Alternative gemstones

Snowflake Obsidian, Eudialyte, Sunstone.

Persevering through challenges Muhammad Ali once said, "I hated every minute of training, but I said to myself, 'Do this now, and you'll be a champion forever.'" And he went on to become the world's greatest boxer. Hold a Preseli Bluestone to help you turn what could break you into the making of you.

PRESELI BLUESTONE

Alternative gemstones

Jasper, Indian Granite, Fire Agate.

improve your mood and mind

BERYL

Quietening racing thoughts When you're finding it difficult to silence the voices within, Beryl is a brilliant crystal to use. Put one under your pillow to clear and quieten your mind, and help you to stop stressing.

Alternative gemstones
Pink Opal, Rhomboid Calcite, Yellow Labradorite.

HOWLITE

Improve your memory More forgetful than a goldfish with amnesia? Place a piece of Howlite on your third eye chakra to boost your memory skills, and ensure you don't forget Aunt Deirdre's birthday again.

Alternative gemstones
Rhodonite, Tourmaline, Emerald.

PEARL

Balance your mood Feeling pricklier than a cactus? Keep a Pearl in your pocket, and rub it any time someone gets your back up to help you stay grounded, and prevent you from throwing a hissy fit.

Alternative gemstones
Chalcedony, Prehnite, Aquamarine.

Instant pick-me-up When life gets tough, pick yourself up by walking away from the drama, and saying a mantra. Find a Black Tourmaline, look in a mirror, and say, "Hakuna matata," which is Swahili for "no worries." You should feel calmer straight away.

BLACK TOURMALINE

Alternative gemstones
Black Agate, Adamite, Jade.

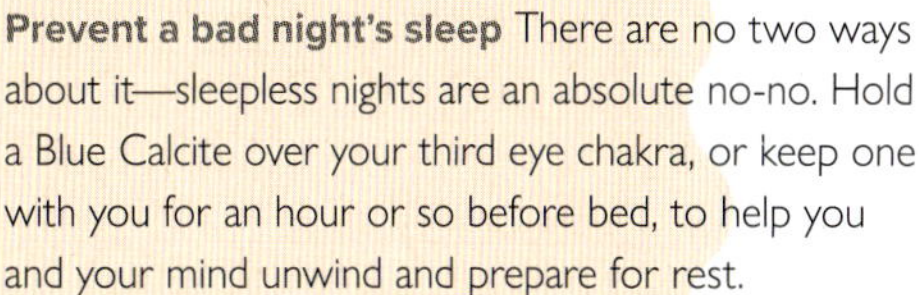

Prevent a bad night's sleep There are no two ways about it—sleepless nights are an absolute no-no. Hold a Blue Calcite over your third eye chakra, or keep one with you for an hour or so before bed, to help you and your mind unwind and prepare for rest.

BLUE CALCITE

Alternative gemstones
Amazonite, Tourmaline, Pink Opal.

Achieve inner harmony Give your mind a rest by placing a Dalmatian Stone on your forehead any time you start feeling exhausted by your thoughts. Imagine the gem absorbing all of your tension, and filling your body with its calming vibration. Then close your eyes and smile.

DALMATIAN STONE

Alternative gemstones
Ametrine, Halite, White Calcite.

nurture your creativity

Singing and dancing, writing, painting—who hasn't wished to be good at one or other of these at some time in their lives? If any or all are a challenge, that's no reason not to try. You can get your creative juices flowing by placing an **Orange Calcite** crystal under your pillow to stimulate your imagination, and ensure you wake up feeling really motivated, and ready for some serious artistic action.

Give yourself a Ginger Rogers-style makeover by wearing a **Carnelian** necklace to boost your performing mojo. It's a great crystal for dancers and actors, and will give your karaoke performances a show-stopping edge, too! However, if you were born with the singing skills of a vocally challenged parrot, you may need to harness your inner disco diva by playing your favorite song and holding a **Kyanite** by your throat to improve your musical abilities, and to help you sing like an angel.

If you long to be a wordsmith, awaken your inner Shakespeare by placing a piece of **Turquoise** beside your laptop or writing journal to unlock your writing talents, and help you weave words together perfectly. And an

CARNELIAN

KYANITE

absolute must for would-be artists is **Picasso Marble**. Place one in your work room to help you see and capture all the beauty around you, and inspire you to share your gift with the world.

ORANGE CALCITE

alternative gemstones

Orange Calcite Fire Agate, Labradorite, Tourmaline.
Carnelian Blue Kyanite, Blue Calcite, Thulite.
Kyanite Rhodochrosite, Rhodonite, Apatite.
Turquoise Citrine, Dolomite, Rose Quartz.
Picasso Marble Celestite, Ametrine, Tiger Iron.

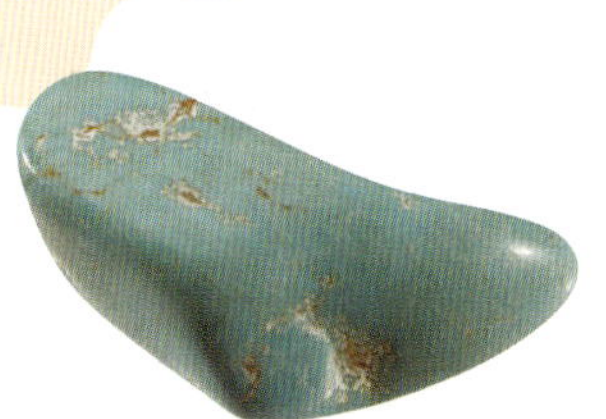

TURQUOISE

PICASSO MARBLE

self-love

MUSCOVITE

Appreciate your beauty Turn your body image from drab to fab by placing a Muscovite crystal on your bedside table to silence the negative voices within, and help you realize how gorgeous you are.

Alternative gemstones
Carnelian, Jade, Magnesite.

THULITE

Appreciate your unique qualities As Buddha tells us, "All of us, as much as anyone, deserve our own love and affection." Heed his wisdom by holding a Thulite gemstone by your heart to help you appreciate your own gifts and beauty.

Alternative gemstones
Titanium Quartz, Obsidian, Larimar.

CHRYSOPRASE

Self-acceptance Holding a Chrysoprase crystal is like having the support of everyone you love in a gemstone. Place it by your heart to help you cherish, appreciate, and accept yourself as much as your closest friends do, and chase away your inner fears.

Alternative gemstones
Stichtite, Pink Kunzite, Eudialyte.

Silence your inner critic There's a bad wolf inside us all—a horrible creature, always waiting for that one chance to spoil our soul's rapture. Hold a Scapolite by your heart to silence the voice of your beast, knowing you and your mind will soon be left in peace.

Alternative gemstones

Black Actinolite, Tourmalinated Quartz, Larimar.

SCAPOLITE

Individuality Oprah Winfrey was once told to change her name to Susie to appeal to more people. She didn't, and went on to become America's first African-American billionaire. Wear an Aegirine to help you see your uniqueness as a blessing rather than weakness.

Alternative gemstones

Diamond, Topaz, Sugilite.

AEGIRINE

Song of yourself There is nothing more unjust than keeping your inner music hushed. Make sure your song lives on by recording your life in a journal. Hold a Septarian while writing the entries each night, knowing that your story deserves to be told, and is more precious than any piece of gold.

Alternative gemstones

Orange Phantom Quartz, Diamond, Yellow Topaz.

SEPTARIAN

PURPLE SCAPOLITE

Positive self-analysis It's often not what others say about us that we fear most, but what we say to ourselves. It's our own critique we're most afraid of. Hold a Purple Scapolite by your heart to help you benefit from your self-scrutiny, and turn your inner bully into a friend.

Alternative gemstones

Peach Aventurine, Mohawkite, Yellow Apatite.

PERIDOT

Be patient with yourself The only person you ever need to be better than is the one you were at your lowest. True success is about progress. It isn't about being the best, or better than the rest, but doing your best. Hold a Peridot to help you remember that.

Alternative gemstones

Rhodochrosite, Mangano Calcite, Tiger's Eye.

Lovely attributes Some gems were traveling from the Sun to the Earth, and collected all of the colors of a rainbow on their way, thus creating Tourmaline. Wear one to help you appreciate the beautiful traits you've picked up on your travels, too.

Alternative gemstones

Goethite, Chrysoprase, Rose Quartz.

WATERMELON TOURMALINE

Self-esteem My favorite quote of all time comes from Oprah Winfrey: "I was once afraid of people saying, 'Who does she think she is?' Now I have the courage to stand and say, 'This is who I am.'" Repeat these words to yourself each and every day, with a Sunstone, until you feel exactly the same way.

SUNSTONE

Alternative gemstones

Lazulite, Pumice, Strawberry Quartz.

Be kind to yourself "Forgiveness is the fragrance the violet sheds on the heel that crushed it." Mark Twain was right. According to myth, these flowers were created when the goddess Diana protected a nymph by turning her into a violet. Hold an Iolite, derived from *ios*, meaning "violet," to heal any self-blame.

IOLITE

Alternative gemstones

Brandberg Amethyst, Rutilated Quartz, Peridot.

Believe in yourself To achieve anything, you need to believe in yourself. Place a plant in your garden with a Stichtite in the pot, to help you sow the seeds of your self-belief, knowing that you will reap happiness.

STICHTITE

Alternative gemstones

Magnetite, Carnelian, Calcite.

POWER CRYSTAL

opal

Star signs Cancer, Libra, Scorpio, Pisces
Planet Venus
Element Water
Chakras Heart, Throat, Crown (varies according to color)

Opals have bewitched us with their mesmerizing beauty for centuries. Steeped in magic and mystery, they are thought to capture the properties of all the gems their colors so exquisitely reflect—they inspire us to be adventurous, like Rubies, loyal, like Emeralds, and kind to ourselves, like Amethysts. Synonymous with empowerment, confidence, and beauty, Opals prompt us to explore the beautiful colors of our inner landscapes and adorn the world with their captivating splendor.

gem-scriptions

Beauty Wear a pair of Opal earrings to bring out your natural beauty, and make you feel like a goddess.
Love Cleopatra is believed to have worn Opal jewelry to bewitch Mark Antony's heart with her beauty. Wear an Opal around your neck to win the heart of your Mark Antony!
Empowerment According to legend, an old Roman senator once chose to go into exile and leave all his possessions behind rather than sell them to Mark Antony—all his possessions, that is, except an Opal. Hold one by your heart to inspire you to stay true to yourself, too.

crystal cocktails

supercharge the gem's power

Opal + **Alexandrite** = maximize beauty and charm

Opal + **Diamond** = develop unshakeable confidence

Opal + **Red Jasper** = witness transformation

ALEXANDRITE

DIAMOND

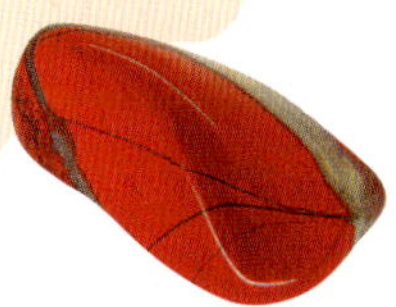

RED JASPER

POWER CRYSTAL

amethyst

Star signs Virgo, Capricorn, Aquarius, Pisces
Planets Jupiter, Neptune
Elements Air, Water
Chakras Crown, Third Eye

The name "Amethyst" comes from the Greek word *amethystos*, meaning "not intoxicated," which is exactly what the gem does for us. Whether our vision of reality is being distorted through a feeding frenzy of toxic relationships, thoughts, and beliefs, or others are spiking our minds with a lethal cocktail of anger, bitterness, and self-doubt, Amethyst is the wise friend telling us we've had enough, and are ready to go home. Teaching us how to feel rich without being rich, love without someone to love, and unite rather than fight, Amethyst is the matchmaker that brings our hearts and minds together, and ensures nothing comes between them.

gem-scriptions

Protection Place an Amethyst crystal by your front door, or hang one on a windchime by your window, to protect your home from negative energy.
Nightmares Put an Amethyst stone under your pillow or on your bedside table to scare away bad dreams.
Toxic thinking Start a compliments journal, and write down anything nice anyone says to you. Read through it with an Amethyst by your heart to remind you how wonderful you are.

crystal cocktails

supercharge the gem's power

Amethyst + **Green Aventurine** = protect yourself from overly demanding friends

Amethyst + **Pink Crackle Quartz** = boost self-image

Amethyst + **Smoky Quartz** = stop yourself falling back into bad habits/relationships

GREEN AVENTURINE

SMOKY QUARTZ

POWER CRYSTAL

carnelian

Star sign Leo

Planet Sun

Element Fire

Chakras Sacral, Root

A gorgeous, "feel-better" stone, Carnelian is an orange variety of Chalcedony that has been prized since ancient times for its ability to bestow courage, energy, and eloquence upon its owner. This captivating gem will give you the self-belief needed to embrace change, live your dreams, and achieve your highest goals. If your spirits are low and you feel lethargic, let high-energy Carnelian restore your vitality and motivation, allowing you to awaken to your true talents and appreciate the beauty around you. Known as the "artist's stone," Carnelian has been associated with the fiery colors of the rising sun for centuries, and encourages us to shine our light brightly, and share our gifts with the world.

gem-scriptions

Improve self-esteem Place a bowl of Carnelian gems in your living room.

Believe in yourself Bury a Carnelian in your garden and watch your self-belief grow, along with your plants!

Protect yourself from negative energy Put a large chunk of Carnelian outside your front door.

crystal cocktails

supercharge the gem's power

Carnelian + **Bronzite** = learn to love yourself and your unique qualities

Carnelian + **Peridot** = enhance your natural charisma

Carnelian + **Blue Kyanite** = tap into your creativity and discover hidden talents

BRONZITE

PERIDOT

BLUE KYANITE

conclusion

So dear reader, here we are at the end of our journey together. When I first started writing this book, I wanted to help you heal, not realizing I'd heal myself in the process. As I wrote about the gems to help you sow, water, and harvest the seeds of romance, friendship, domestic bliss, career success and, most importantly, self-love, I grew a garden myself. I found my soul mate (this book), weeded out the bad seeds in my friendship circle and planted new ones, and became closer to my family than ever. The day I finished my last chapter, I felt like I'd lost a dear friend, only to bump into my new neighbor for the first time. Her name is Jade (the stone of friendship).

I hope the rituals and crystals in this book bring you as much joy, happiness, and hope as they've brought me, and have inspired you to see the rose quartzes in every garden, gold in both your own and other people's hearts, and silver lining to every cloud, so you can look in the mirror, and wholeheartedly love, appreciate, and marvel at what you see.

I also hope you'll write to tell me about your wonderful crystal experiences. I'd love to read your crystal stories so please do email me at to_gol@hotmail.com, find me on Facebook (@golnaz.alibagi), or follow me on Instagram (@naz_alibagi), where you can read more of my crystal tips and follow my crystal adventures.

And just in case you need proof of how magically powerful crystals can be, here's a little anecdote to strengthen your faith further. When I was about 13, I used to go into a wonderful spiritual shop every day after school. My parents didn't have much money at the time, so I couldn't afford to buy anything; but each day without fail I'd go into my little magical sanctuary, and admire all the beautiful gemstones. One day, when no one was looking, I held one by my heart and wished I'd get a book published by the time I was 30 and a diamond necklace from Tiffany & Co. at some point in my life. My book went to print two weeks before my 30th birthday. And my gift? A diamond necklace from Tiffany & Co.

stockists

Best Crystals
www.bestcrystals.com

Charms of Light
www.charmsoflight.com

Coleman's Crystal Mines and Rock Shop
www.jimcolemancrystals.com

Crystal Cure
www.crystal-cure.com

The Crystal Garden
www.thecrystalgarden.com

The Crystal Healer
www.thecrystalhealer.co.uk

Crystal Vaults
www.crystalvaults.com

Earth Gallery
www.earthgallery.com

Exquisite Crystals
www.exquisitecrystals.com

Healing Crystals
www.healingcrystals.com

Mineral Miners
www.mineralminers.com

Peaceful Mind
www.peacefulmind.com

resources

Cassandra Eason, *Crystals for Passion and Romance* (Seven Oaks, 2014)

Cassandra Eason, *The New Crystal Bible* (Carlton Books, 2010)

Denise Whichello Brown, *The Power of Crystals* (Bookmart, 2002)

Doreen Virtue & Judith Lukomski, *Crystal Therapy* (Hay House, 2005)

Judy Hall, *101 Power Crystals* (Fair Winds Press, 2011)

Judy Hall, *Crystal Love* (Godsfield, 2008)

Judy Hall, *Crystal Prosperity* (Ivy Press, 2010)

Judy Hall, *The Crystal Bible* (Godsfield, 2013)

Judy Hall, *The Encyclopedia of Crystals* (Godsfield, 2013)

Mary Lambert, *Crystal Energy* (CICO Books, 2010)

Michael Gienger, *Crystal Power, Crystal Healing* (Cassell, 2002)

Michael Gienger, *Purifying Crystals* (Findhorn, 2008)

Philip Permutt, *The Crystal Healer Volume 1* (CICO Books, 2007)

Philip Permutt, *The Crystal Healer Volume 2* (CICO Books, 2018)

Philip Permutt, *The Modern Guide to Crystal Chakra Healing* (CICO Books, 2021)

Simon and Sue Lilly, *The Essential Crystal Handbook* (Duncan Baird, 2006)

Simon Lilly, *Crystal Healing* (Element, 2002)

a–z of crystals

Here is a catalog of the crystals featured in this book, including the pages they appear on and their associated star signs and chakras (the body's energy centers—see opposite). It can be helpful to work with the crystals that are most associated with your star sign, or with the chakra you feel you may need to work on.

THE CHAKRAS AND THEIR ASSOCIATIONS

Crown (top of head):
Spiritual connection, awareness, knowledge, and inner peace.

Third Eye, also called Brow (between the eyebrows):
Intuition, psychic abilities, imagination, and inspiration.

Throat (center of throat):
Communication, self-expression, truth, and listening.

Heart (center of chest):
Love, relationships, compassion, and connection.

Solar Plexus (upper abdomen):
Confidence, personal power, willpower, and motivation.

Sacral (just below navel):
Creativity, confidence, sexuality, and pleasure.

Root, also called Base (base of spine):
Stability, grounding, security, and feeling safe.

B

D

T

acknowledgments

First and foremost, I'd like to thank my beautiful little sister, best friend, and favorite person in the world Mahsa, who—like the moon she was named after—has always brought light into my darkest moments, and supported me more than anyone during the writing of this book. I'd also like to thank my amazing mum and dad, who came to Britain with nothing and still gave me and my little sister the best childhoods we could have hoped for; thank you for never giving up on me, and showing me the true meaning of unconditional love.

I'd also like to thank CICO, and the amazing Cindy Richards and Lauren Mulholland, for taking a chance on me, and helping me turn my dream into a reality; thank you for making the reality of my dream even more wonderful than I'd imagined it would be. I'm also very blessed to have many, many close friends (they know who they are!), and would like to thank them for celebrating my happiness with me, and cheering me on every step of the way.

I'd also like to thank the wonderful writers—particularly Judy Hall, Cassandra Eason, Phillip Permutt, and Mary Lambert—whose books have inspired me so greatly, and who I've learnt so much from.

And last but not least, I'd like to thank you, dear reader, for believing in me enough to pick up this book, and loving yourself (and my words) enough to read it to the last page.